SHARING JOY'S TREASURES

an exquisite antique shell collection
reveals hidden stories

CHRISTINE ROBINSON

Author: Christine Joy Robinson

ABN: 30645130454

Email: crobinson8@bigpond.com

Facebook: Christine Robinson

Instagram: Christine Robinson

Copyright ©:

First Published: 2020

ISBN: 978-0-6450501-5-8

DEDICATION

In celebration of my mother, Joy,

and

nature's exquisite treasures

CONTENTS

PREFACE

This is a story about a timeless family heirloom, a precious treasure capturing the essence of nature's beauty and was inspired by my love and appreciation of seashells, nature, family, history and antiques.

Come on a journey, nearly 200 years in the making, as I sprinkle a bit of magic from my childhood and explain how I discovered letters and documents, hidden within a collection of antique shells and natural specimens. This treasured heirloom has allowed me to explore the lives of the characters involved, and the threads that connect two families. It offers more questions than answers. It adds layers of intrigue and invites us to peer into shallow rock pools and to immerse ourselves in the wonders and mysteries of deep oceans. It is a reminder to appreciate the beauty that surrounds us, and to look beneath the surface, because you never know what you might reveal.

Writing this book has triggered memories of my childhood and wonderful carefree days at the beach with family and friends. It also inspired me to investigate the historical references and the fascinating stories that emerged from the depths of a cabinet of curios, and enticed me to visit faraway places, to explore their origins.

This story honours the memory of my dear mum, Joy, whose presence, influence and loving kindness hold a special place in my heart. It is the perfect way to celebrate a lifetime of love and the cherished moments we shared, appreciating the exquisite beauty of this stunning collection.

I am blessed to be the custodian of my mother's most-prized possession, a treasure chest filled to the brim with nature's gifts. The beautiful treasures, not only touched the core of my soul but they also enhanced my innate love of our natural environment and reinforced the importance of protecting and conserving our precious ecosystems. This exquisite collection has captivated my imagination throughout my entire life; but little did I know, the treasure chest had more to reveal.

It is a privilege, to share the images in this book, to showcase the magnificent colours, patterns, textures and designs of these amazing creations of nature. My thanks for the mastery of Sonja Wrethman, a professional photographer on the Sunshine Coast, who listened to my ideas regarding composition, and who captured the macroscopic details in some of the images, and highlighted their unique features. I wish to acknowledge the Reverend Joshua Tinson, and my great grandfather, Ernest Henry Pretyman. They gathered the approximately five hundred shells and natural specimens and stored them within the drawers of an antique cabinet, ensuring these treasures were protected to this day.

FOR EVERY JOY THAT PASSES
something beautiful remains

My mother was born in Hobart, Tasmania in 1927, to Ernest 'Roy' Pretyman and Kathleen (the daughter of Joseph and Emily Bidencope). Her birth name was Kathleen Joy, but everyone called her Joy. The definition and meaning of the word 'Joy' in the Collins English Dictionary is 'a source or cause of keen pleasure or delight; something or someone greatly valued or appreciated' and reflects how everyone felt in Mum's presence, with her warm personality and happy disposition.

This story is a personal tribute to my dear mum, who by her own example showed us the joy of friendship, the spirit of generosity, the beauty of love and how to care deeply about the well-being of others, with compassion and kindness. Mum taught my older sister, Anne, and I invaluable life lessons including gratitude, patience, acceptance, trust, resilience and courage. She was a gracious lady, who instilled the rules of social etiquette in us, as well as the value of respecting others and the importance of expressing our sincere thanks for kind gestures and thoughtful gifts.

Mum was admired and respected in her community, and was fortunate to have enduring friendships, many of which she nurtured since childhood. Mum and her friends were a great support to each other throughout life's challenges. Mum loved the sport and camaraderie of lawn bowls, and during her fifty-year association with the local club, she was awarded Life Membership. She also enjoyed the fellowship, the informative guest speakers, the social interaction and the activities, as a member of the local Probus club, and these social events offered her a certain 'joie de vivre'. She cherished her role as 'home manager' and dedicated her life to creating a loving and comfortable home for her family.

My parents loved each other deeply, and complemented each other with many shared interests. My dad, Ray, was my hero and a wonderful role model who possessed admirable qualities such as—integrity, courage, bravery, selflessness, humility and patience. As a family, we enjoyed many adventures, exploring the idyllic natural environment of our island state creating many precious memories I hold dear.

When he was a young man in Tasmania, my father contracted poliomyelitis, during the 1937-38 epidemic; however, he recovered, with minimal residual effects, after several years of rehabilitation. Unfortunately, the early years of his working life exposed him to the perils of asbestos, and many years later a diagnosis of mesothelioma ended his life too soon.

My paternal grandfather died, when I was a little girl. He left a lasting impression on me; with his snowy-white hair, his blue-tinted glasses in thick black frames, and the tapping sound that echoed from the long, white cane he used to guide him, as he was visually impaired. The most significant impact he had on my young life was through his simple gift of a book, called *Tinka and His Friends* by Brownie Downing and John Mansfield.

This enchanting children's story about an Aboriginal boy living in the bush with his native animal friends, inspired my love of literature. It taught me that books have the power to transport us to another time and place, to captivate our imagination, and to take us on an adventure, without leaving home. The beautiful foreword of this book still resonates with me today:

'When a child is born there is a corner in its heart which is magical. Some children discover this magic and keep it all their lives; others must be shown; and there are some who never find it. Many lose it all too soon, to re-discover it again in old age. It is for all those who have found the magic, for those who have lost it, those who seek it, and those who have never known it, that we write this story.'

I was blessed to have discovered a magical world within a treasure chest, containing an exquisite shell collection, and it has enchanted me all my life.

A few years ago, I entered a Mothers' Day competition at a local fashion store. They posed the question, 'Tell us why your mum has made you the woman you are today'. My response was, 'My Mum is a wonderful friend, and her generous spirit has shown me the value of respect, and the importance of making a difference in our community. She reminds me to be grateful for simple pleasures, to appreciate the little things in life, and live our lives with integrity, grace and wisdom. To see the beauty in the world, value our freedom and independence, have the courage to pursue new challenges and adventures, and to follow my heart. I treasure the moments we shared, and how she has influenced my life to be the best person I can be. I am proud to be my mother's daughter'. My simple declaration of who my mother was won me the competition!

Mum loved writing letters. It was part of her daily ritual and she often signed off with the word *Mizpah*; a protective and endearing expression, representing a symbol of affection. In Hebrew, it means watchtower and is a reminder that one is always loved, no matter whether you are together or apart. In 1979, while I was living in Wimbledon in London, a silver Mizpah brooch caught my eye in the window of an antique shop. I knew it was the perfect gift for Mum, as we never parted without expressing our love for each other.

Mizpah brooch

During the years that I spent away from my mother, residing overseas and interstate, I looked forward to receiving her informative letters she sent each week. Before posting each one, she would apply a fresh coat of lipstick and kiss the envelope to leave a clear impression of her lips. This gesture was always a welcome sight when I found a letter from home in my letterbox.

When Mum's health deteriorated and she required assistance with activities of daily living, I decided it was time to return to my birthplace to care for her. It was the least I could do, and a small way to repay her for the unconditional love and support she had so generously given me, my entire life. She expressed her wish to stay in her beautiful home as long as possible, and as a retired nurse I had the experience to adapt to her changing needs, and was in a position to provide the love, support and care she required.

Mum loved to reminisce about the people who had played a significant role in her life, the places she had visited and the memorable events she had attended that held fond memories for her. I am thankful I had the foresight to make a recording of a few of these conversations. Mum also shared memories of her childhood and family folklore. These personal accounts about our ancestors, and their lives and relationships, are a valuable record of our family's history and heritage. It has also been helpful in piecing together the history of the family heirlooms I was fortunate to inherit.

This photo of the Pretyman family was taken in 1884, in the garden of Queenborough House in Sandy Bay, Hobart where generations of my family had lived for well over a century. My great grandfather, Ernest Henry Pretyman, is standing at the back of this photo, on the right, with his penny-farthing bicycle. The year this photo was taken was a significant one for my family. Amongst my mother's papers, I discovered evidence explaining how a woman, unrelated to my family, had bequeathed her father's collection of shells and seed pods to my great grandfather in 1884, when Ernest was just nineteen years old.

Pretyman Family - Queenborough House - Hobart Town 1884

Ernest added to this collection extensively, during his lifetime, and the shells and natural specimens he had acquired were kept in several large cabinets and drawers, as well as being displayed on shelves. Following his death, in 1941, my grandfather donated the larger specimens in the collection to the local museum. He received a letter from the director who asked, 'In the event of our not wishing to retain the entire collection, what would you like us to do with them?' I distinctly remember Pa telling us how disappointed he was with this response, considering his father had devoted many years of his life to acquiring the vast array of shells for his collection. Pa's response was, 'Throw them back into the sea, where they came from'. To this day, I wonder whether they did.

In a handwritten note, my mum explained how 'This collection of shells, seeds, eggs and other natural specimens housed in a beautiful rosewood cabinet was a very small part of my grandfather E.H. Pretyman's collection I inherited when I was thirteen years old'. Every time we drove past my great grandfather's family home, Mum and I would say aloud, and in unison, 'Thank you Grandpa', to express how grateful we were for this magnificent collection, as it has given us countless hours of pleasure.

Mum was always respectful and careful about how she handled the shells. To my knowledge, she only ever viewed them as they lay on the surface of their cotton wool beds, occasionally nudging one back into place if it had moved from its designated position. Despite having viewed the collection many times, during her lifetime, Mum had no idea of the fascinating stories and letters hidden beneath the surface of the compartments, within this cabinet of curios.

We experienced great sadness as the essence of our mum slowly slipped from our grasp. Nothing could prepare us for the deep sense of loss and the cavernous space her passing created, after she died on July the 14th 2015. I miss our long conversations, holding her in a warm embrace, touching her soft skin, feeling the beat of her heart, and her comforting touch that reminded me how much I was truly loved.

Following Mum's passing, I returned to Queensland, to enjoy the unsurpassed beauty of the Sunshine Coast and to adjust to life without my dear mum. I knew the expanse of the ocean, the stunning beaches and the vibrant tropical environment would soothe my soul and make my grief and loss more bearable, or – at least – a little easier.

The tide recedes, but leaves behind
bright seashells on the sand.

The sun goes down but gentle warmth
still lingers on the land.

The music stops and yet it echoes on
in sweet refrains.

For every joy that passes
something beautiful remains.

Martha Vashti Pearson

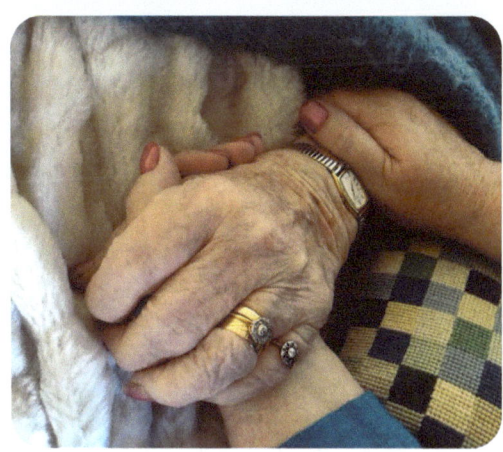

CABINET OF CURIOS

every shell has a story

My love affair with this collection began when I was just a little girl. The first time I viewed the display of nature's treasures, it stole my heart and I have been inextricably invested in and emotionally connected to the cabinet of curios ever since. I am in awe of the magical world of seashells and the beauty of each unique specimen, with its stunning pattern, colour and intricate details.

My great grandfather recognised the importance of protecting the specimens from excessive handling and exposure to light, heat and dust; so, he stored them within the drawers of a cabinet. This demonstrates how much he valued the collection and his intention to preserve the specimens for future generations to enjoy. Thanks to his care, most of these creations of nature have retained their original colours and structural integrity.

My sister and I spent many hours with Mum, spellbound by the splendour of these natural creations, and we listened intently as she shared her childhood memories of the collection. Mum loved to visit her grandfather, as he had an entire room dedicated to his collection of shells. She often recalled her excitement at running up the stairs to stand on her tippy-toes and peer into the large drawers and cabinets; so, imagine her delight when she inherited this collection.

We affectionately referred to this collection as Mum's 'treasure chest'; an apt description, because it contains an impressive display of shells, natural specimens, gems and artefacts. Today, it is a valuable representation of the depth of our love, as well as a tangible memory of the cherished time we spent together. The simple action of pulling out one of the drawers evokes sentimental feelings and, at times, I am instantly transported back to the innocence of my childhood.

As children, we loved having friends visit our family home, so we could share the contents of Mum's cabinet of curios, and her ritual of exposing each of the six layers of her treasure chest, one drawer at a time. We gathered around the cabinet and as Mum slowly pulled out the bottom drawer, we leaned in for a closer look, peering in to study the shells that were laid out in seven neat rows on large sheets of cotton wool. After scanning the contents in this first layer, Mum would place her hands at either end of the tray, grab the indentations in the wooden frame and lift the tray out to reveal 93 different shells, also laid out in neat rows beneath it.

We always respected Mum's request to 'look, but don't touch', even though I was always bursting to get my hands on them. So, it was a rare treat when she gave us permission to reach in and pick up a shell, from its nest in the cotton wool. I would hesitate for a brief moment, aware these treasures were fragile and needed to be handled with great care. I remember what a thrill it was to hold one of these precious shells in my hand, and how proud I felt as I lifted it up in the air to point out the beautiful features to my friends.

As we viewed each drawer, and its different specimens, with their vast array of colours, shapes and patterns, I drew my friends' attention to a few features and told them the names of the shells I knew.

The patterns and textures of some of the shells are quite remarkable, with their intricate surfaces and structures. The stages of growth, revealed in the lines in the mantle and the whorls visible on the surface, show how the shell expanded in size, to accommodate the animal as it grew inside. We often pondered about the creatures that once inhabited the inner sanctum of these empty exoskeletons and what their life was like under the sea.

One drawer contained seedpods, bird skulls and other specimens, not found in our local environment and we were intrigued about their origins. We spent a significant amount of time examining the contents of the next couple of drawers, which held around 200 specimens, and as Mum placed them back into the cabinet, I found it hard to contain my excitement.

After viewing the contents of five layers of the cabinet, it was now time for the big reveal: the very top layer of the cabinet. At this point, I would usually remark with great enthusiasm, 'Wait until you see what's in this drawer'. As much as I loved every unique shell in the collection, the top layer was always my favourite and, even today, I never tire of gazing at the *pièce de résistance* of the entire collection.

15

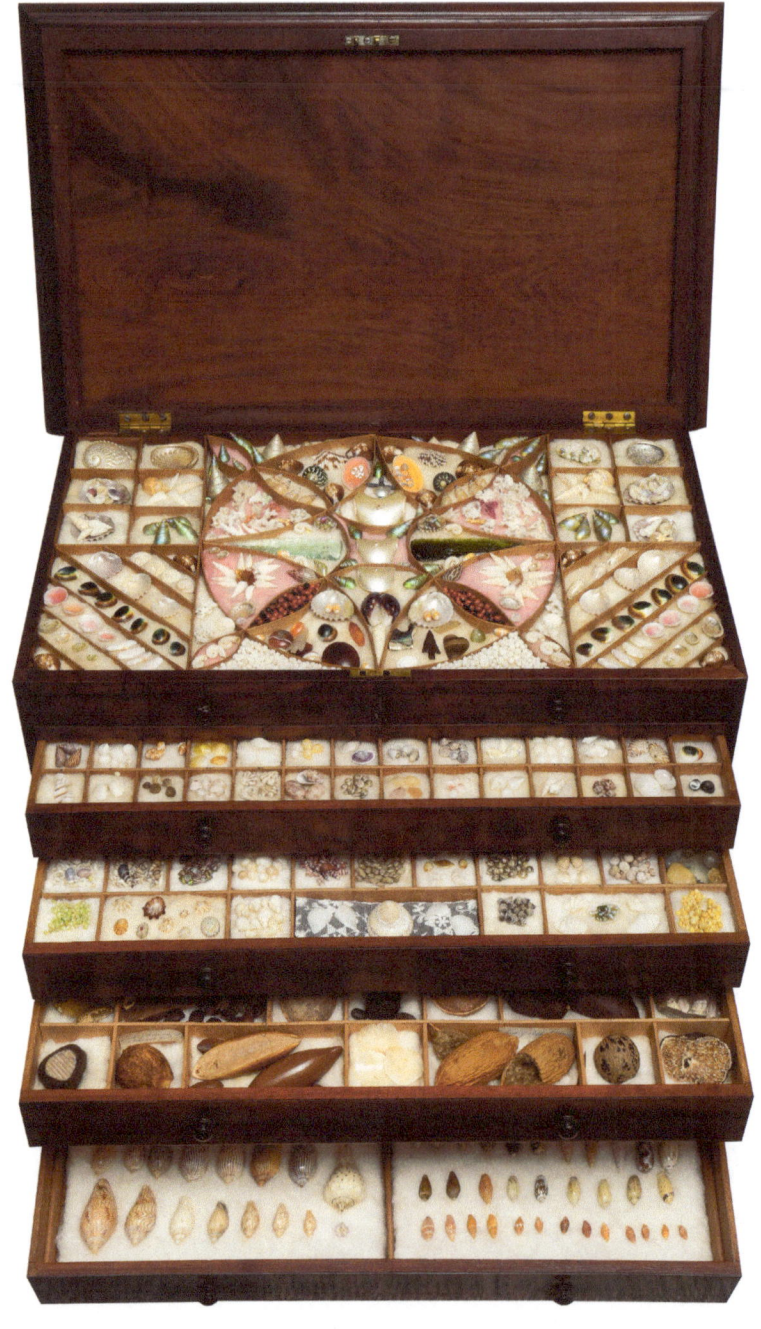

We held our breath in anticipation as Mum reached for the tiny knobs, to extract the last drawer, but it would not open and we all let out a deflated sigh. Mum would tease us by reaching for the little key and Anne and I would play along with Mum's ploy, expressing our disappointment, 'Oh Mum, is that all there is?' As we reluctantly moved away from the cabinet, Mum carefully removed the antique silver picture frames, small glass perfume bottles and other interesting keepsakes she displayed on top of the cabinet.

She would turn around and look into our faces, smile, and ask if we were ready to see more. Of course, there was always an enthusiastic response in the affirmative.

Mum slowly lifted the lid of the cabinet from the front edge with great aplomb, and the exquisite layer on top was finally revealed. It was a sight to behold. I would loudly exclaim 'ta-da', as I felt this moment deserved a theatrical introduction, and the unveiling was usually met with 'oohs' and 'ahs', as our friends gazed at the incredible work of art laid out before us. The expression of pure delight on our friends' faces was priceless, and I always felt like the luckiest girl in the world. Sharing this precious treasure has always been a privilege.

To appreciate the dimensions of the cabinet, and to put the minute size of some of the specimens into perspective, know that it measures 66.5 cm x 45 cm x 38 cm. Mum told us the cabinet was made from rosewood, but the small turned drawer knobs are of a darker-coloured wood. I have viewed every surface of the cabinet, but there are no visible markings or labels to identify the craftsman or offer clues as to its origin. The drawers and the lid appear to be made of three different types of wood and the rich hues, colour tones and character change when viewed in different lights and angles.

Before moving it from Tasmania, I prepared the collection by covering the surface of each drawer with a fine layer of fabric and securing the edges to create a snug fit. I did not entertain the idea of removing all the shells, as I didn't want to disturb the ordered arrangement of the specimens. The cabinet was then wrapped in a thick bundle of felt blanket, and stickers applied to alert the couriers this was 'fragile' cargo and needed to be handled with great care. Stickers with arrows were also applied to 'Keep this way up'. I wished it safe passage, crossed my fingers that the cabinet would arrive in one piece and resigned myself to finding a few of the specimens out of place, when it arrived at my home in Queensland.

It took fourteen days for the cabinet to travel from Hobart, Tasmania, across Bass Strait to the mainland and on to my new home in Noosa Heads on the Sunshine Coast. I had already decided on the perfect spot for it, where it would take pride of place. I was overjoyed at the prospect of viewing this precious collection once again.

I was totally unprepared for the distress I experienced, when I opened the first drawer. I let out an audible gasp and exclaimed 'Oh no' aloud, as I surveyed the dishevelled mess that lay before me. My worst nightmare had actually happened, as only a few of the shells remained in their designated positions. The fact this had happened on my watch was upsetting, as I had always respected the precise order and arrangement of the specimens. I felt as if I had let Mum and my great grandfather down, by not protecting this family heirloom. My immediate reaction was to close the drawers, to avoid looking at the mess. It could wait until I was in the right frame of mind, to begin the daunting task of returning each specimen to its rightful place.

I knew the process of sorting the shells would take countless hours of patience and persistence. The next day, I was ready to begin the restoration and I made a commitment not to give up until I was satisfied the collection resembled the original display. I was determined to honour the legacy of the original collectors, who had created this magnificent exhibit. I scanned the contents of each drawer and realised, with relief, that only a few shells had suffered irreparable damage. Their delicate structures had been reduced to small fragments and, unfortunately, I had to remove them from the collection, which resulted in a few empty compartments.

I gathered all my strength and patience, took a deep breath, let it out, and began the onerous process of sorting the cabinet one shell, one section and one drawer at a time. Luckily, I had taken photos of the six layers in the cabinet's five drawers, several years earlier, which proved to be an invaluable reference, to guide me through the restoration.

I decided to approach the process as Mum would have done and began with the bottom drawer first. This drawer contained the larger specimens and I figured it would take less time to place the shells back in order and, thus, I would actually feel as if I was making progress.

I placed the drawer on my kitchen bench, switched on the lights and devoted what seemed like a thousand hours to carefully picking up each specimen from the layers of cotton wool and placing them together according to their appearance, size and common group, until I was ready to return them to their original position.

There are thin strips of wood at each end of the base of the bottom drawer, and one in the centre, all of the same height. They are designed to prevent contact with the shells below, and allows the thin tray, containing 153 smaller specimens, to sit on top of the bottom layer, within the same drawer.

Numbers are written in black ink, on the top edge of the wooden compartments, within three of the drawers, indicating that my great grandfather had possibly compiled an inventory and recorded the details and classification of each specimen. Unfortunately, Mum had no knowledge whether a catalogue existed, as it was not part of her inheritance.

Over the next couple of years, the restoration project occupied many hours each day and it opened up a new avenue for researching the historical records that I discovered under the layers of cotton wool. It also changed my perception of the contents of the cabinet. Whereas previously I had focused on it as a thing of beauty, I now gained knowledge and insight into the complex world of shells and the other artefacts. I could appreciate them for the wonders of nature that they truly were, and for the fascinating history of their origins.

WHAT LIES WITHIN
the treasure revealed

The first layer that I tackled, in my mission to re-establish the cabinet, contained shells classified as gastropod molluscs. It included olive shells *Olividae* (carnivorous sand burrowing marine snails). These cylindrically shaped specimens ranged in colour, from vibrant, shiny orange carnelian, with distinct white stripes, to a speckled, brown pattern and a few have a pale cream background. As I turned over the tiny yellow oliva tessellata shells, with their dark, muted pattern of dots on the surface, I was surprised to see a vibrant shade of purple lining the opening, or aperture, of each shell.

First layer

There are a few 'lettered olive' specimens. They are the shells of a predatory sea snail and are distinguished by their elongated, cylindrical shape and the small spire at one end. They come in different colours and tones and have a unique zigzag, hieroglyphic-like pattern with scribbled lines, which accounts for their name.

I developed a newfound respect for the sea snail specimens in the collection, with their distinctive shapes and amazing variations in size, colour and texture. Some have a glossy sheen while others are matt and textured; there are even a few translucent specimens. It is incredible how these delicate shells have not decomposed over time.

Researching the lifecycle of these specimens has been fascinating. During the early stages of development, some snail shells undergo an action known as torsion, where the mass inside the shell and the shell itself twist $180°$, from facing to the rear to facing forward. This action of torsion (usually to the right), gives the shell the characteristic spiral direction that is specific to some species of snail. Until I began researching these shells, I had not considered that a large number of shells in this collection were those of marine snails.

Bottom drawer

'There are 93 specimens in the base of the bottom drawer. Some measure 7 cm in length and these images show the unique characteristics of each specimen.

The whelk shell in this collection has small brown speckles on the surface. During my research to identify the species, I came across images of egg casings. These plump discs make up a long strand of segmented pouches, referred to as a 'mermaid's necklace'. In its natural form, one end of the spiral of egg capsules is secured with mucous to the ocean floor or to a rock, and acts as an anchor, preventing it from being washed away. When the babies (protoconch) are ready to hatch, they escape through a hole in the casing.

Whelk shell and juvenile whelk snails

The juvenile snails hatch, fully formed, in the shape of the mature whelk shell and develop the features of the adult shell, later. I discovered that the little white shells, I had placed with the tiny green shells, are in fact, juvenile whelk shells. The green shells are a species of sea snail, called Emerald Nerite shells, *Smaragdia viridis*. They are gastropod molluscs in the Neritidae family of saltwater and freshwater snails. Other members of the Neritidae family, include the Clithon oualaniense and Green Tiger Nerite seen in the open section of the oyster pearl shell, image #15 indicating their size in comparison to the pearls. Some nerite snails have distinct zigzag, chevron patterns and striations on the surface.

*Emerald nerite/Smaragdia viridis
in a limpet shell and white
juvenile whelks*

*#15 Black nerites, yellow Clithon
oualaniense, zebra nerite, Bullina
virgo, two natural pearls and Beau's
vitrinella in open oyster shell*

Indian volute: Melo melo   *Mitra mitra*

Mitra stictica and mitra   *Auger shell*
mitra

The bottom drawer contained a wide variety of shells, including the volutidae/volute species.

Voluta musica

Amoria zebra

Cymbiola vespertilio

Cymbiola pulchra woolacottae

Pseudonebularia
pediculus

The next drawer I tackled, in my quest to restore the cabinet to its former glory, highlighted the depth of the collection. Wonders from the land such as the specimen that resembles a petrified truffle (tuber) #26 are displayed side by side with the fascinating marine life, which also includes a section of petrified barnacles (crustaceans).

A variety of shells in bottom drawer

Petrified barnacles

#26 This specimen resembles a petrified truffle

The central section of this drawer contained a large eggshell and two smaller eggshells, with the number 200 written on the surface in black ink. There are three small bird skulls and three bird's nests with twigs and seeds woven into their soft structures, to create a cavity for a small species of bird.

Leaf with 'South Africa 1916'

This central section also held a small, pale-grey leaf with the year 1916 and South Africa handwritten on its soft furry surface. It is possible that my grandfather obtained this during his service with the AIF in WW1, and thereafter added it to the collection.

Pink sea urchin spine

Purple sea urchin spine

This drawer held three different types of sea urchin spines that looked like thick blunt spikes made from a single crystal of calcite, a mineral consisting of calcium carbonate. A finely woven pattern is evident on the larger vibrant-purple specimen, when it is viewed from an angle where direct light falls onto the surface. The smaller, deep-pink spine has a tiny pattern of raised circles covering two thirds of its length and a striped pattern at the other end.

Blister pod Sacoglottis amazonica and Manchineel Hippomane mancinella

Sea beans/Mucuna urens/Hamburger beans

Macadamia integrifolia seeds

Cashew nuts

Nutmeg seed with mace covering (aril)   *Caster beans*

Eucalyptus pods and acorn caps

Sawtooth oak acorn Quercus acutissima

African dream herb seed Entada rheedii

Vegetable ivory: tagua nut

Manicaria saccifera: Sea coconut top

Manicaria saccifera: Sea coconut base

Curled piece of wood

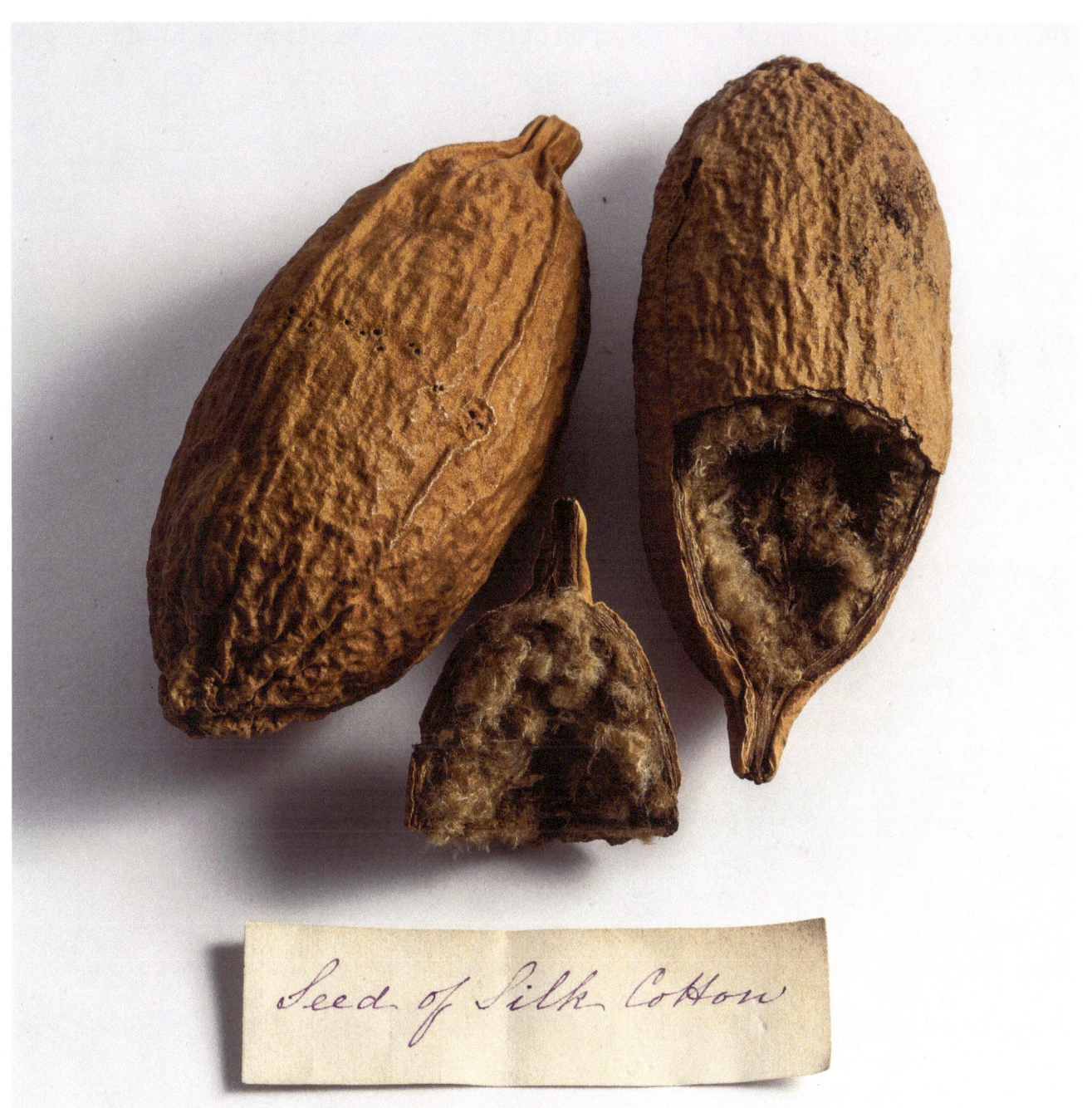

Seed of Silk Cotton

43

There are several specimens that I couldn't identify, but these images are worthy of inclusion as they demonstrate the variety of unusual specimens in the collection.

The drawer holds several quandong seeds, which have a tough, pitted outer surface. The Desert Quandong (or wild peach) features in Aboriginal bush tucker cuisine. Two seeds in this collection have been shaped to represent a basket, and another has a handle and an intricate pattern carved into the seed's side and base. The deep-purple-toned berries, with their wrinkled and aged surface may in fact also be from the quandong family, as they have the appearance of red Desert Quandong fruit in its ripened state.

The Blue Quandong *Elaeocarpus angustifolius* is a rainforest tree, native to Australia, also referred to as the 'Blue Marble Tree'. The seed that is found in the blue orbs has a woody endocarp with more protrusions than the smooth surface variety of Desert Quandong: *Santalum acuminatum.*

Imfibinga seeds, also known as Zulu teething beads or Job's tears, are pale blue and grey seeds that originate from Africa. These droplet shaped seeds have often been used to make jewellery.

Desert Quandong seeds:
Santalum acuminatum

Imfibinga/Job's tears/
Zulu teething beads

Purple seeds, possibly dried Desert
Quandong fruit

Blue Quandong Elaeocarpus
angustifolius

Abrus precatorius

Red Lucky Seeds
Adenanthera pavonina

The striking bright red seeds with a black section at one end are the *Abrus precatorius*, also known as rosary pea or giddee giddee. They are one of the most poisonous seeds known to man, but only release their toxin when the seed is broken.

As we viewed the collection, over the years, we often unfolded the thin strips of paper that were tucked down the side of a few of the compartments, to read the handwritten descriptions of several specimens. After further investigation, I discovered that the handwriting belonged to the original collector, Reverend Joshua Tinson, as the style of writing on these labels matched the letters I discovered in the base of the compartments, underneath the shells.

I found one piece of paper with an interesting looking nut label, describing it as a 'kernel of serpent nut'. I have been unable to find any image or reference to this nut, but assume it could be related to a Jamaican fruit, as Joshua Tinson lived in Jamaica for many years.

Nicker nuts

Seed of Mammy Sapota (sic)

These images are specimens identified by Tinson in his handwriting.

The mamey sapote *Pouteria sapota* is a fruit and this specimen is from Jamaica.

Nicker nuts or sea pearls are seeds that grow in prickly pods on a climbing shrub. They grow wild on the beaches of the Caribbean islands, and are often used to make necklaces and bracelets.

The water caltrop, sometimes referred to as the water chestnut, is a bizarre fruit. It has two prominent horns and has a woody, sculptured surface that resembles a face, or the head of a bull.

Hawaiian baby woodrose *Argyreia nervosa* is a climbing vine whose seeds are enclosed in a furry pod and contain naturally occurring tryptamine, called LSA (Lysergic acid amide), which is closely related to the hallucinogen LSD.

The West Indian Locust is a hardwood tree, common in the Caribbean. It produces a seedpod that is referred to as Stinking Toe Fruit, as it resembles the shape of a big toe and has an unpleasant odour when the fruit is ripe. The hard fruit pods contain edible dry pulp that surrounds the seed inside. The resin of the *Hymenaea courbaril* tree, is called animé, and used for varnish, perfume and incense.

Hawaiian baby woodrose seed Argyreia nervosa

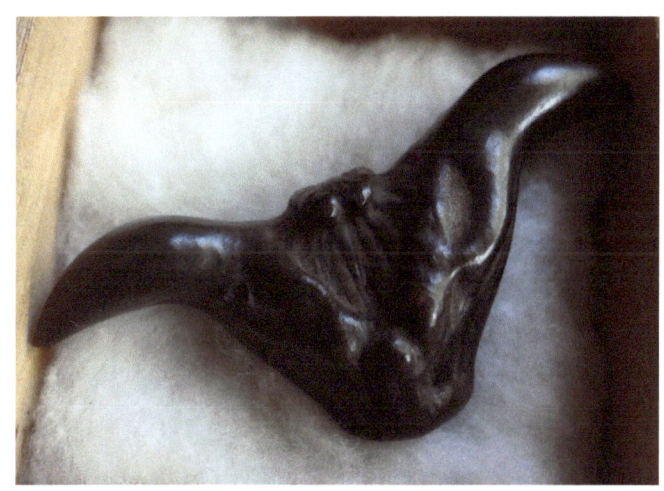

Water caltrop Trapa bicornis seedpod

West Indian Locust Hymenaea courbaril seedpod

Aleurites moluccanus: candle nut: Kukui nut & Manicaria saccifera pod

The *Aleurites moluccanus:* candlenut: kukui nut is also known as a Jamaican walnut, because the wrinkled surface of the nut resembles that of a walnut.

Sea sponge

This thin, pale-yellow specimen has a small tuft at the base and a larger head of fine threads at the top. The smaller end allows the sponge to attach to another surface, to provide an anchor, while the fine tendrils are designed to waft to and fro in the currents, waiting to envelop smaller prey as they drift past.

This drawer also contained a fingernail shell, or a minor jackknife clam, with a pink and white striped pattern that reveals the stages of its growth, as well as a thin cross section of a conch shell. There are a few gemstones, including one that looks like natural carnelian—its red colour indicates trace amounts of iron.

Third drawer

Goose barnacles Lepas anatifera

The goose barnacles *Lepas anatifera* were often out of place, when we opened the third drawer and despite my pulling it out carefully, these specimens caught on the frame of the cabinet as it was withdrawn. Thus, a few were broken and needed to be removed and replaced with other specimens. Given their fragility and age, I am thankful only a handful of the specimens were damaged.

The third drawer, and the specimens in disarray,
after the cabinet arrived from Tasmania

In the original display, the brown felt always attracted cotton wool fibres, so I decided to cover these sections with some pieces of antique cream lace I had found in a workbox that once belonged to Joshua Tinson's wife, Eliza. When I removed the documents and memorabilia from the bottom of the workbox, I found a brown oyster shell with a rough outer surface that was secured with clear sticky tape. I removed the tape, which revealed a pearly white nacre lining and, to my surprise, two glistening natural pearls.

This discovery created the perfect solution for one of the empty spaces in this drawer. I placed the open shells in the space, from where I had removed the damaged specimens. I positioned the shells on top of the lace, with the lustrous mother of pearl facing upwards, and placed the natural pearls in one-half of the shell. The other half of the shell was the perfect home for a few tiny specimens and would demonstrate their size, and highlight their unique features, alongside the pearls.

Natural pearls in shell

Tiny specimens in oyster pearl shell

Pink tellin shells

Olivella biplicata: purple dwarf olive, cowrie shells, and jackknife clam shell

Umbonium vestiarium, Common/
Vesta's Button Top and thomasi snail
shells on $1coin

Banded kelp:
Bankivia fasciata shells

Blue sea snail on limpet shell

Cerithium vertagus shells

Keyhole limpet with red spot, true limpets, cockle shell and kitten's paws

Polygyra cereolus, Zethalia zelandica, Common violet, and Discus rotundatus snails

The *Polygyra cereolus* snail shell is flat, with about eight whorls. It resembles a coiled rope with distinct ridges and a flared aperture in the shape of a heart. The wheel shell *Zethalia zelandica* is a species of sea snail. The common violet snail *Janthina janthina* has a pale spire and a deeper colour on the ventral side. They secrete a mucous called chitin, from a gland in their foot, and trap air bubbles, created by agitating the water. The surface then hardens to form a sort of raft, so they can float upside down on the surface.

The first three layers had required methodical sorting to return the shells and natural specimens to their correct positions and arrangement according to the original display.

The next two drawers of the collection captured my attention by revealing their hidden secrets, in the form of letters and newspapers, to add another dimension regarding the history of the contents of the cabinet, and offered me a deeper appreciation of the collectors' efforts.

The second-to-last drawer was divided into 112 compartments, and it contained the majority of the smaller shells. These specimens had suffered the most significant disruption during transportation. Only a few shells remained in their original locations and the rest were a jumbled mess. It required many hours of picking up each one with a pair of tweezers, to return them to their common groups. I placed these tiny specimens in empty egg cartons, small cups, liqueur glasses and any other small container I could find. When I placed the shells back on top of the cotton wool layers, in their original compartments, I took photos to share with my family.

When I looked closely at these images, I noticed small pieces of broken shells and dark fibres embedded within the layers of aged cotton wool, and although they were not obvious to the naked eye, I decided this restoration project was worthy of attention to detail. I lifted each square segment of cotton wool out from the compartments, one by one. Using a magnifying glass and a pair of tweezers, I painstakingly removed each fibre and fragment of shell until I was satisfied the cotton wool was free of foreign material.

Third drawer restored

Trocomorpha shells

Pyramid periwinkles Nodilittorina pyramidalis and Cantharidus pulcherrimus

Phasianotrochus bellulus, Phasianotrochus eximius and Cantharidus pulcherrimus

During the process of cleaning the cotton wool, I discovered folded sections of newspaper and letters, which had been packed into the base of each compartment to provide a foundation for the shell collection. The stacks of paper varied in height, which was important to create a uniform level, so that the tops of the specimens sat below the top of the wooden frame when the drawers were opened and closed; thus protecting the shells from potential damage.

As I carefully unfolded each piece of paper I realised I had come across a second, or buried, treasure within the cabinet. The words written on these pages revealed intriguing references to history and transported me back in time. Small advertisements in the pages of newspapers from Jamaica, England and Tasmania, depicted issues of the era and reflected the conditions, lifestyle, attitudes, language, expressions, words, and distinct styles of communication.

As soon as I released these historical documents from the depths of the cabinet, their snippets of information revealed threads that tied this story together. With each discovery, I experienced an overwhelming sense of excitement. I decided to photograph the documents for future reference, as I wanted to continue the process of restoration. I meticulously folded each piece according to its original creases and returned them to the base of each compartment, where they had been placed originally. I put the layer of cotton wool back on top, so each shell would be in its original space. In some sections, I used the underside of the aged sections of cotton wool, to present a more pristine surface that enhanced the overall beauty of the display.

Despite the distress I experienced when I discovered the jumbled mess of shells and artefacts, and the significant disruption to the ordered arrangement of the collection, I am thankful for the situation, as it proved to be a blessing in disguise. I was rewarded with the discovery of intriguing stories and an opportunity to expand my knowledge about the history and origins of each specimen. After delving into every corner of each drawer, to search for more information, I felt a deeper personal connection to this magnificent heirloom, and the intrinsic value of the collection was enhanced.

Mussel Clam Abalone Oyster Bivalvia, black abalone, Stomatella impertusa

Trochus shells

Blue pink gold lined pipi and clam shells

White Tridacna crocea clam shells, trochus and rainbow kelp shells

Pink top shell
Clanculus dunkeri

Cone shells

Spondylus gaederopus oyster and Chlamys rubida scallop

Hydatina amplustre

Bivalve, zigzag clam with purple lining

Scallop shells

Top shells Gibbula umbilicalis

*Trigonia Neotrigonia margaritacea,
ribbed top shell and green abalone*

Mulberry whelks Tenguella granulata

Annularia fimbriatula

Moon snails   *Naticarius onca moon snail*

Green and knobby white sea urchins   *Annularia fimbriatula*

*Jingle shells/mermaid's toenails,
from the family of saltwater clams*

*Baby's Ear Moonsnails:
Sinum perspectivum*

*Bivalve with zigzag pattern
(holes created by a moon snail)*

Pink tapestry: Turbo petholatus

During the period that the collectors accumulated these shells, they used whatever resources were available to them, as a foundation for the specimens. These included pieces of newspaper, copies of letters cut into pieces, woven strips of ribbon, and other unidentified material. At first glance, I had thought that the compacted wads of brown fibre that I found were made from the outer husk of a coconut, but on closer inspection, they actually resembled human hair!

The pages of personal correspondence and the information contained within the pages of newspaper were no doubt deemed insignificant at the time, but have since proved to be valuable documents, as they enabled me to confirm provenance. The newspaper clippings and handwritten letters were far more than simple scraps of paper. They unearthed the origin of the collection and provided valuable information about the connection between the Tinson and Pretyman families. As well as explaining my own connection to Reverend Joshua and Eliza Tinson, they told how their story and the collection formed a significant part of my own history.

My curiosity was piqued by the style of language and the words that were used to express opinions or situations in these letters and sections of newspapers from the colonial era and this inspired me to document my findings. As I pieced the information together, I discovered just how far the collection had travelled, and how it had found its way to me, via Jamaica, England and Tasmania.

Now, the mere act of touching these treasures, somehow offers me a tangible connection to family members, who cherished the collection. As I hold them in my hands, I can almost feel the energy of the gentlemen, who carefully collected and preserved these treasures.

Revealing stories and material used as foundation in the compartments

Drawer with the 112 compartments restored

My great grandfather enhanced the collection by adding shells, unique to Tasmania, and these complement the other objects in the top layer. No doubt, the intricate pattern he created to accommodate the various sizes and shapes of the specimens required significant planning. Thin pale strips of wood create curves for each section in this central design. These curves form an impressive frame for displaying the shells, and I have often wondered what inspired this artistic addition.

The most significant shapes in this pattern were created on either side of the central section, to house two glass spears, known as Kimberley points.

Kimberley points were created from European bottle glass discarded by the early settlers. The local Aboriginal community, in the Kimberley region of Western Australia, used the glass to shape spearheads for hunting. The distinctive and uniform pattern denotes the skill and precision of an indigenous craftsman, who applied precise pressure and a forceful movement from a pointed stick or shaped animal bone to flake out the surface of the glass. Kimberley points have sharp, serrated edges on both sides and a very sharp point. They were attached to the end of a wooden shaft with twine, and were often secured with heated resin. These artistic and ingenious tools, crafted from material that had been discarded by the white settlers, were a desired artefact for collectors of souvenirs and curiosity items.

Kimberley points

Materials found under Kimberley points in the top layer

Killiecrankie diamonds

Killiecrankie diamonds are a colourless variety of topaz, found on Flinders Island, and hand crafted to resemble true diamonds. These gems epitomise the beauty found in modern diamonds. The collection contains a few uncut, clear and pale-blue water-worn specimens. The pink lining of the tellin clam shell provides a perfect backdrop for the six Killiecrankie diamonds and highlights the unique qualities of these old European-cut 'diamonds'. Even though they do not have the precision or brilliance of modern diamonds, they still possess a timeless romantic quality.

Moonstones: a natural crystal mineral

Moonstones are cabochons with a flat base and a domed surface that accentuates their adularescence. They are transparent and from certain angles have a floating blue tone, which creates a mysterious shimmer of light and the impression of lunar light floating on water. They have characteristic inclusions, such as tiny tension cracks called centipedes, and crystal formations. These frozen moonbeams symbolise new beginnings, strength and inner growth. Placing the moonstones in an orange tellin shell perfectly balanced the Killiecrankie diamonds in the pink tellin shell.

The Pearly nautilus *Nautilus pompilius* is a cephalopod/mollusc related to the squid and octopus and the only animal in this species that has a visible shell. It has a fleshy hood, which acts as a trapdoor that seals off entry to the shell and protects the animal, which withdraws when predators approach.

There are four sections of the nautilus, arranged in graduated sizes, as a feature in the centre of the top layer. Thus far, I have not located any images in other collections that show this particular perspective of the complete septum, with unique patterns etched into the surface of each one.

I purchased the nautilus shell in images #109, #111 and #112 from a local vendor, on the beach in Bali, Indonesia, in 1978. While on holidays in Port Douglas a few years ago I found the cross-sectioned specimen and it was a meaningful gift for Mum. Both of these specimens were useful additions to our collection, as they allowed us to show friends where the four sections of septa in the collection were positioned within the nautilus shell.

I love the exposed iridescent nacre, or pearly surface, of the nautilus shell, after it has been hand polished to remove the outer coating, and how the curve glistens as light is reflected on the surface. It highlights the natural, striped markings and the subtle, pastel colours that shimmer and glow as the light changes throughout the day.

The nautilus septa provide partitions that separate each compartment and, as the animal grows inside the shell, it moves forward into the next, much larger chamber that has formed. The growth of the nautili, and increasing size of each chamber, provides buoyancy, through the exchange of gases and water, via the siphuncle. This is a strand of tissue, formed as a tube, which passes through each section of the nautili, via the holes visible in the centre of each septum. Nautili have survived for more than 500 million years and are considered living fossils.

#109 Nautilus (from author's personal collection)

#111 Nautilus, cross section and antique septum with engraved pattern

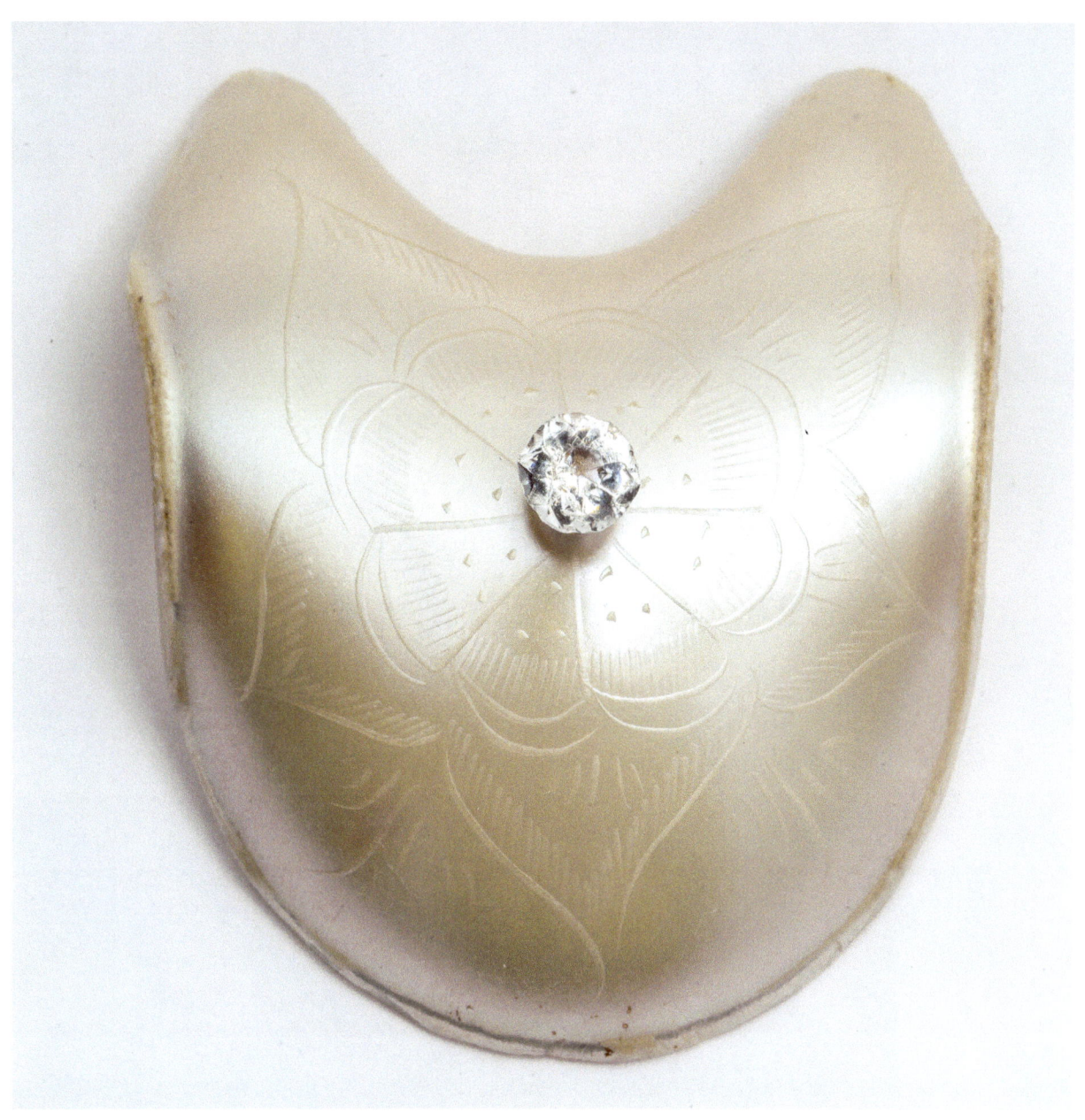

#112 Nautilus septum with Killiecrankie diamond sitting in the siphuncle notch

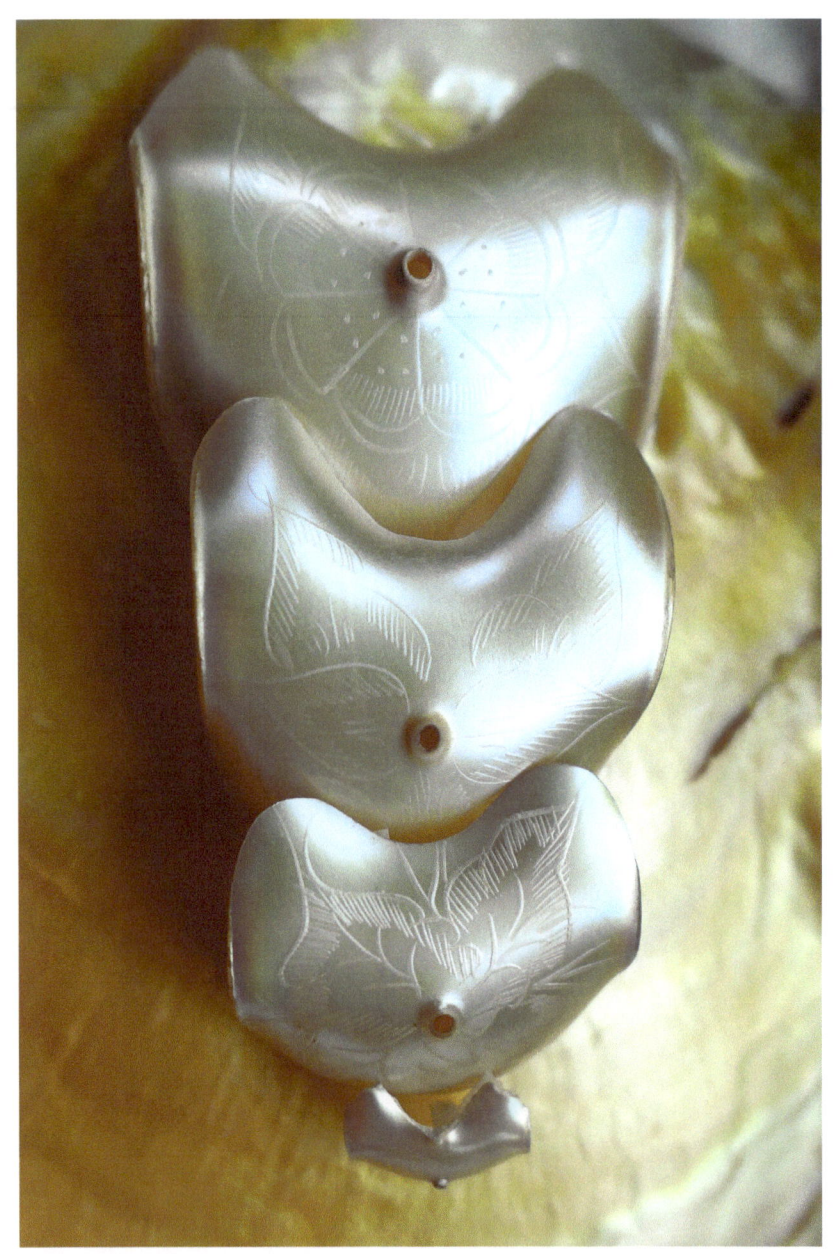

Four sizes of nautilus septa with engraved pattern

Spirula spirula

The white spiralling specimens are the internal shells of the Ram's Horn Squid *Spirula Spirula* and are a species of cephalopod. They have similarities to the nautilus shell, as they are made up of several chambers that constitute a buoyancy organ, to help the animal orientate itself in an upright position, while keeping the body vertical.

Maireener shells have a strong connection to indigenous culture in Australia; but sadly, they are becoming rare. Today, only a few women seek them the traditional way; standing in icy cold water at low tide, to reach below the surface, grasping lengths of kelp to locate the attached shells, before carefully removing them. At this point, the shells have a brown coating, which requires an acid solution to expose the hidden opalescent colouring.

I loved capturing the iridescent qualities of these King Maireener shells, as the vibrant blues and greens were highlighted and varied in intensity with different lighting, and when viewed from different angles. It is a privilege to have a few of these beautiful shells in my collection.

Renowned Aboriginal artist, Lola Greeno, and her family are dedicated to preserving indigenous tradition and culture through their use of Maireener shells. They honour the historical significance and the skills of generations of indigenous women from Tasmania's Cape Barren and Flinders Island.

Maireener Phasianotrochus irisodontes

Souvenirs of Tasmania

Many years ago, my grandfather, Ernest Roy Pretyman, donated 2000 glass plate negatives to the Tasmanian State Archives. One of the images in the Pretyman Family Collection (NS1013/1/1871) is dated 1898. It concerns souvenirs of Tasmania, and was designed and manufactured by A. Butterfield, a local Tasmanian jeweller. This image shows how local shells, such as the Maireener, Trigonia margaritacea and Phasianotrochus irisodontes were used to craft 'souvenirs' during this era.

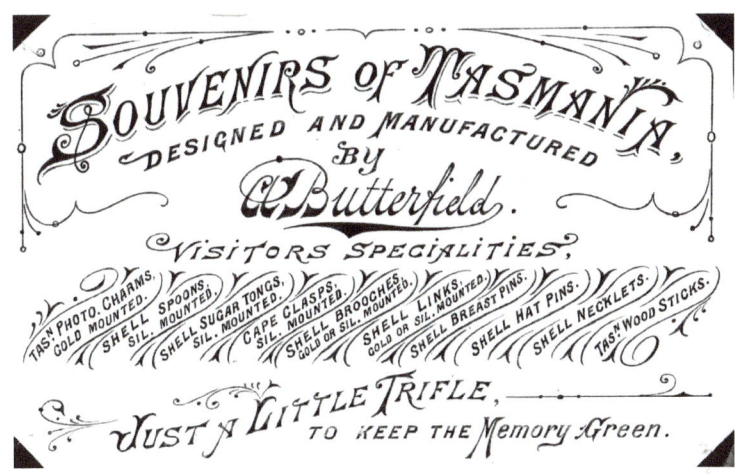

Souvenirs of Tasmania A. Butterfield 1898

Maireener (rainbow kelp shell)

Maireener shells

Coral specimens

Trigonia shell with rainbow kelp shells

Trigonia shells containing: Spirula spirula, wentletrap, tiny starfish, cowrie and Epitonium varicosa

Trigonia shells with ridged surface

Abalone shells

Operculum from the Cat's Eye Turban: Turbo petholatus, plus a green Chrysoberyl 'Cat's Eye' gem stone

Crucifix made from lava stone originating from Mt Vesuvius

Scallop and ribbed pecten speciosum

Trochus niloticus

Blue Mussel shells (with number 287)

Green Turban Shell

Sea biscuit with five radials

Snake Head
Cowrie

Tellin

Killiecrankie Diamonds

Moonstones

Crucifix (Lava from Mt Vesuvius)

Scallop

Engraved Nautilus Shell Septa x 4 sizes

Maireener

Green Turban

Periwinkle

Maireener

Coral

Trochus Niloticus

Iridescent pink green
blue & purple
Maireener shells

Coral

Phasianotrocus
bellulus

Kimberley
Points

Abalone

Phasianotrochus
eximus

Cerithium
eburneum

Abrus
precatorius

Orange carnelian
olive

Sea biscuit

Neontrigonia
Margaritacea

Spirula
spirula

Mother of Pearl

Orange Agate

Blue Mussel

Arrow Head

Trivia

Brown Agate

Carnelian from Lake Superior

Cerith

Paua

Chrysoberyl Cat's Eye

Identification of specimens in centre of top layer

101

The exquisite display in top layer

The circular design in the centre of the top layer has become my personal mandala and it provides a focus for contemplation and meditation, as I find the exceptional beauty of these natural creations is mesmerising and has the power to calm my mind and provide a sense of peace.

Centre of top layer

Side panel top layer

Side panel top layer left side

Side panel top layer right side

EVERY CLOUD HAS A SILVER LINING

Joshua and Eliza Tinson

The saying 'every cloud has a silver lining' comes to mind, when I reflect on the circumstances that led me to discover the fragments of letters and newspapers, discretely hidden within the layers of my antique cabinet. It is possible that these fragments of history might have remained buried under the display of shells forever, had I not had cause to restore the collection.

The documents are a reflection of history, which transported me back in time to the colonial era, where this collection began, and they provided me with substantial evidence to confirm the provenance of the items in the collection. I was able to identify the specimens Joshua Tinson collected between 1822 and 1850, while he lived in Jamaica and also determine which specimens my great grandfather, Ernest Henry Pretyman, had contributed to the collection, after he acquired it, in 1884. I learned about the lives of Reverend Tinson, the original creator of the collection, and his wife, Eliza, who took a leap of faith when they moved from England to Jamaica as Baptist missionaries.

As I unfolded each piece of paper and examined the details, I wanted to understand more about their lives and to explore how we were connected. I had always been curious about the faces that stared back at me from the miniature portraits my mum kept in a workbox, and I often wondered about their relationship to my family.

Reverend Joshua Tinson was born in Gloucestershire in 1794, and he entered the Bristol Baptist College in 1818, as a missionary student. In 1822, he did not hesitate when asked to respond to an urgent need for a missionary in the West Indies and accepted this as his ultimate calling. In February 1822, he married Elizabeth Haines, also a native of Gloucestershire. In March of the same year, he was ordained into service as a Baptist missionary and, on March the 24th, they departed England for Jamaica. They travelled by sea for several weeks, before reaching their destination, a town in southeast Jamaica called Morant Bay.

Their arrival on this small island must have been overwhelming for them, as they adjusted to not only life as a newly married couple but also a new country that was vastly different to their homeland. They had to assimilate unfamiliar cultural traditions, learn a new language, experience a new food culture and understand differing beliefs.

While I was researching Joshua Tinson, I discovered the book, *The Voice of Jubilee*, which includes a chapter about Tinson's character, his life and commitment to his faith and his work as a missionary. The authors, and fellow Baptist missionaries, describe how Tinson influenced the lives of the Christian community, and spoke of his significant contribution as a Baptist missionary in Jamaica. Reading about their untiring commitment to promoting their faith and offering education and their contribution to the cause of social justice, during this period, was enlightening.

Joshua Tinson is described thus:

> *'rather tall in stature, but of slender frame and delicate constitution, with a sallowness of complexion that indicated disease. His countenance had a rather melancholy cast, except when engaged in lively conversation, when his features displayed great sprightliness and pleasantry.*

> *He seemed designed for a contemplative rather than an active life; and his circumstances in his latter life especially favoured his natural disposition. He was a man of peace, at the same time tenderly sensitive to unkindness and injury.*

> *He had considerable humour, and was naturally satirical and witty; but these faculties, so often dangerous to the possessor, being under the controlling influences of religion, were seldom employed in a manner offensive or unpleasant; they rather rendered him additionally interesting as a companion and friend.*

> *He was distinguished for habits of early rising, of order, and regularity; nor did he less excel in his love of neatness and cleanliness. All these qualities were visible in his person, dress, house, garden—indeed, were apparent within the sphere of his control, and exerted a widely beneficial influence on his pupils and on the humbler classes of his flock.*

He studied the Scriptures in their original languages critically, and the Sacred Book was by darkness and by daylight his constant companion. He also obtained very considerable knowledge of science in general, and displayed a keener taste in its pursuit than perhaps any of his missionary brethren. His knowledge on almost all subjects, if not profound, was extensive and correct, for he had not only read extensively and carefully, but digested the subjects of almost every book he could procure, whether of divinity, poetry, or general literature. Mr Tinson was not, therefore an ordinary character.

Piety was his principal characteristic, while his faith stood not in the wisdom of men but in the power of God. His piety was the diamond in the circle of his excellences that shed around its sparkling lustre; it shone like a rainbow on the darkened cloud.' (pp 178-179)

I am grateful for this detailed and respectful account, which is evidence that Reverend Joshua Tinson was held in high esteem by his fellow missionaries, and the local Baptist community in Jamaica.

As I read the letters and newspaper clippings, and discovered more about the lives of the collectors, I made parallel discoveries about the history of the times when they accumulated the specimens in this cabinet of curios.

In 1823, Reverend Tinson and Eliza welcomed a daughter, Eliza Helah, in Kingston, Jamaica. The story documented on a piece of paper, found behind Eliza senior's portrait indicates that Eliza Helah was their only surviving child. In the same year as Eliza was born, the British Government made a pledge, regarding the adoption of measures concerning the abolition of slavery throughout the British Empire. The legislation was not passed until 1834, and despite the Abolition Act, the enslaved did not achieve full emancipation from the British Empire until 1838.

In 1829, Eliza returned to England with her mother. She stayed at a boarding school, with Maria Saffery, a teacher and the wife of a pastor, who ran a school for missionary children whose parents were living in various parts of the British Colony.

In 1829, Reverend Tinson travelled extensively through several American states, but then he returned to England, because of ill health, where he remained for several months. Once he had recovered, he travelled around his native land, preaching for the mission, before returning to Jamaica once again. The Tinson's settled in Yallahs, a town located on the southeast coast, which was the site of the first Baptist church in Jamaica.

In 1837, his health deteriorated again and Reverend Tinson travelled back to America, where he spent about five months. Following this trip, he returned to Jamaica to take up a post as the esteemed pastor of the Baptist church at Hanover Street, Kingston, where he remained until 1841. At that time, his health failed again and he decided to give up his position and return to England with daughter, who was eighteen years old, and his wife.

In 1843, the family returned to Jamaica. The Baptist Missionary Society in London had appointed Reverend Tinson as the first President of the Calabar Theological College in Rio Bueno, on the north side of the island. This was to be his final post, before he died in 1850 at the age of 56, after 35 years dedicated to the missionary service.

One of the wonderful discoveries I made were incomplete handwritten letters on pale blue and yellow paper that were hidden beneath the shells. I located two pieces of matching blue paper, and as the words flowed from one piece to the other, they revealed a consistent thread of conversation. This sparked an almost frenzied attempt to find any other pieces of correspondence on pale-blue and yellow paper, so I crossed my fingers and hoped I would find the remaining portions of the letter hidden under other sections within the drawer.

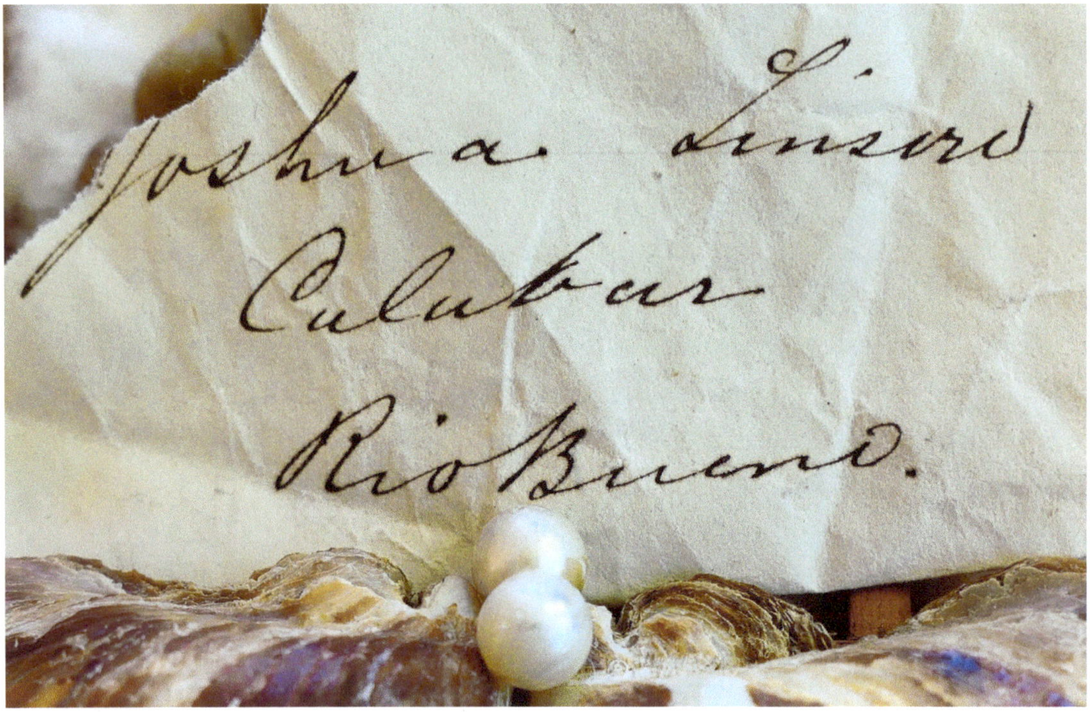
Joshua
Rio Bueno.

Third drawer, with stacks of paper, wherein I discovered pieces of 1837 letter and stories in remnants of newspaper in the base of the compartments

Piece of Gibraltar Rock — & Operculum from Fiji

It was an exciting moment, when several pieces of pale-blue paper revealed words that continued the thread of correspondence, and came together to form a complete letter, consisting of four pages, filled with amazing detail. This letter appears to have been a draft copy and could account for the letter being cut into small sections of paper, to use as packing material to create the foundation for the display of shells within the compartments of the drawers.

While Joshua Tinson travelled to America, his wife, Eliza, stayed in Jamaica and he wrote informative and endearing letters to her. I can sense the love he felt for his wife and daughter, within these pages, through the carefully chosen words he used to express his feelings and his descriptive accounts of his experiences.

Discovering these handwritten letters allowed me to compare them with the style of writing on the thin strips of paper, used as labels for some of the specimens. The sections of letters that were written and signed by Joshua Tinson helped identify the particular specimens he had collected in Jamaica, between 1822 and 1850.

Although Tinson's handwriting is quite legible, it took me a while to interpret some of the words, as I had to adjust to the use of an elongated letter 's', that looks like the letter 'f' without the crossbar, next to a lower case 's' in words such as kisses, illness and sickness. In some cases he uses a descending 'd' at the end of a word; e.g. prepared and acquainted, but not all words ending in 'd' had a descending stroke. I am fascinated by the old English text and the words he used to express a sentiment, as well as how his letters included respectful comments to convey his thoughts and opinions.

This letter was written during Tinson's visit to Philadelphia, and is dated the 22nd July 1837.

Page 1

My dearest Eliza,

Though I have just sent off two letters for you and daughter, I shall commence another that I may avail myself of the earliest opportunity of sending it, and that you may know how I get on. I am sure you will be pleased to learn that my health is improving, and that I am received by the friends here with the utmost kindness and respect. My old friend Colgate from New York has called upon me this morning to know when I will favour the friends in his city with a visit, and wishing to engage me a Sabbath for their large church, and also to attend an Anniversary meeting of 2 or 300 students at one of their colleges in the State of New York. Instead of three months I need to ?value (unable to interpret this word), to meet the wishes of the friends I already know, I suppose the number will daily increase.

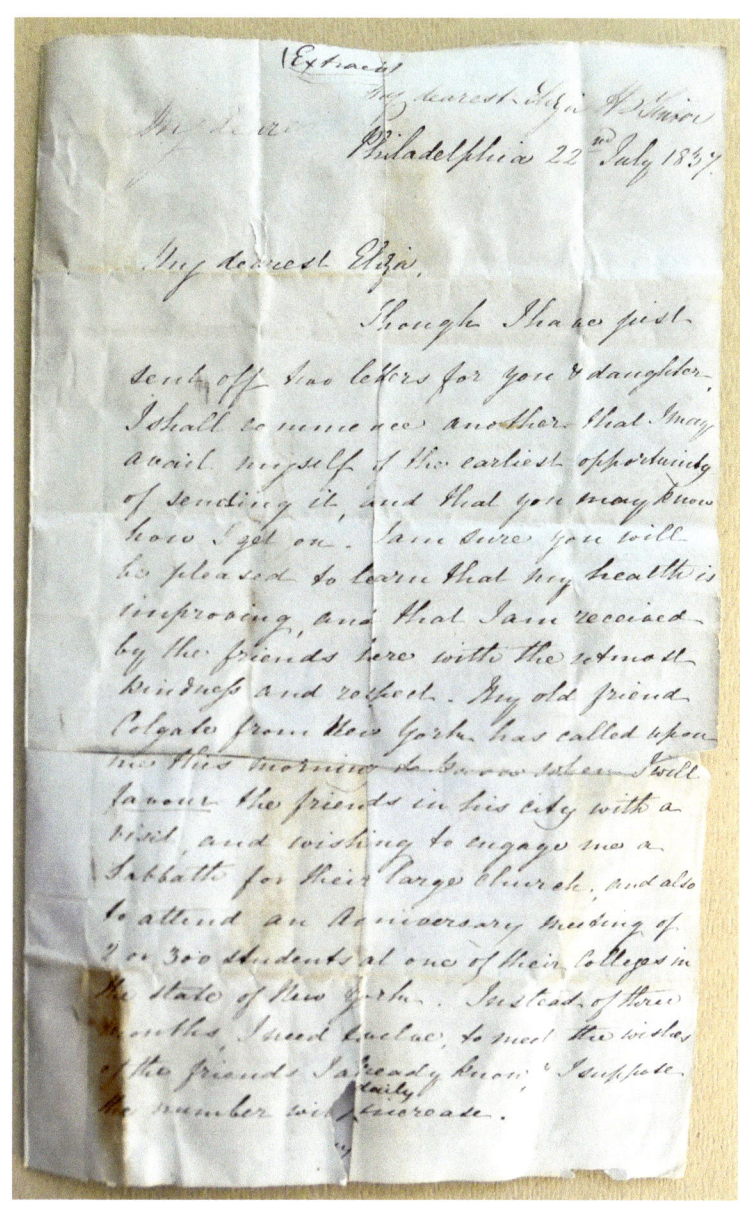

(Extract)

My dear ...

Philadelphia 22nd July 1837

My dearest Eliza,

Though I have just sent off two letters for you & daughter, I shall commence another, that I may avail myself of the earliest opportunity of sending it, and that you may know how I get on. I am sure you will be pleased to learn that my health is improving, and that I am received by the friends here with the utmost kindness and respect. My old friend Colgate from New York, has called upon me this morning to know when I will favour the friends in his city with a visit, and wishing to engage me a Sabbath for their large Church, and also to attend an Anniversary meeting of 2 or 300 students at one of their Colleges in the state of New York. Instead of three months, I need twelve, to meet the wishes of the friends I already know, & I suppose the number will daily increase.

Page 1 of Joshua Tinson letter written to Eliza in 1837

117

Page 2

Baltimore Thursday 27th

Come hither yesterday, and now want to chat a little with my dear wife, how is she? How is my beloved daughter? How gets on the church etc? But who is to answer me these questions? Alas! No-one at present. I am often thinking about the health of yourself and our dear child. Do take care of yourselves. My health is improving. My sight is still weak, but my appetite is very good. Friends are kind, but one must get acquainted with American manners or sometimes the mind would be offended. I am now with a Deacon Crane and his family - they received me very kindly, and they are kind and the family seem anxious to do everything to please me.

Friday August 11th

On Sabbath the 30th I preached in this place (Baltimore) Monday I started for Washington in company with the Reverend Mr Allen & Miss M Crane, daughter of the gentleman at whose house I am staying. We had a pleasant ride in the steam cars; I went to Dr. Chapin's, President of

Baltimore - Thursday 27th. Came hither yesterday. and now want to chat a little with my ~~beloved~~ dear wife - how is she? how is my beloved daughter? How gets on the Church &c? But who is to answer me these questions? alas! no one at present. I am often thinking about the health of yourself and our dear child. Do take care of yourselves. My health is improving, my sight is still weak, but my appetite is very good. Friends are kind, but one must get acquainted with American manners, or sometimes the mind would be offended. I am now with a Deacon Crane and his family - they received me very kindly, and they are kind - & the family seem anxious to do everything to please me.

Friday August 11th — On Sabbath the 30th I preached in this place (Baltimore) Monday I started for Washington in company with the Revd Mr Allen & Miss M. Crane, daughter of the gentleman at whose house I am staying. We had a pleasant ride in the Steam Cars, I went to Dr Chapin's, President of

Page 3

Columbia College, where I was kindly entertained till my departure on the Wednesday following.

Tuesday the 1st August was quite a gala day with your husband - a day spent in viewing the wonders in the City of Washington, and also in George Town, in company with two Misses Chapin, and Miss Crane.

On Wednesday the 2nd August, we went on board the Steamer at Washington, and proceeded down the Potomac towards Virginia - we had a delightful sail some 140 miles and were just on shore about 6 o'clock in the evening; we had then 12-15 miles to go in a small canoe; this we performed in the small space of 5 hours! arriving at our lodgings by 11 at night. Here we were kindly received and entertained by a regular Virginian farmer, whose corporeal dimensions reminded one of Ogg King of Bashan, his hospitality too was of the same character. (I have determined Og, king of Bashan was related to the last race of giants and apparently measured ten - twelve feet, and was taller than Goliath the most well known giant referred to in the Bible). The next morning we proceeded to the camp ground, a distance of about 15 miles, here we stayed buried in the depths of the forest till the next Wednesday when we took our leave of a people whom I in all probability shall never see again; but many of whom I cannot but

Columbia College, where I was kindly
entertained till my departure on the
Wednesday following. Tuesday the 1st
of August was quite a gala day with
your husband. a day spent in viewing
the wonders in the city of Washington,
and also in George Town, in company
with two Misses Chapuis, and Miss Crane.
On Wednesday the 2nd of August we went
on board the Steamer at Washington,
and proceeded down the Potomac
towards Virginia. we had a delightful
sail some 140 miles, & were put on shore
about 6 oclock in the evening, we had
then about 12 or 15 miles to go in a small
canoe. this we performed in the small
space of 5 hours! arriving at our lodgings
by 11 at night. Here we were kindly
received and entertained, by a regular
Virginian farmer. whose corporeal dimensions reminded one of Og, King of Bashon,
his hospitality too was of the same
character. The next morning we proceeded
to the Camp ground, a distance of about
15 miles, here we stayed buried in the
depths of the forest till the next Wednesday
when we took our leave of a people,
whom I in all probability shall never see
again; but many of whom I cannot but

Page 3 of letter

121

Page 4

remember with esteem.

In daughter's letter I shall endeavour to give some description of the camp &c.

Philadelphia 17th August I am again in this place - returned yesterday. Should I not be able to finish my journal up to date for daughter, I will endeavour to send it from New York. I have not time to write brother Gardner- my love to him and wife.

I must now conclude this hastily, as my friend Dr Brantly has been occupying a good piece of my time. A heap of kisses to my beloved daughter and spare her of a long letter in a week or two. May the best of heavens helpings attend you both, is the prayer of

Your ever affectionate J. T.

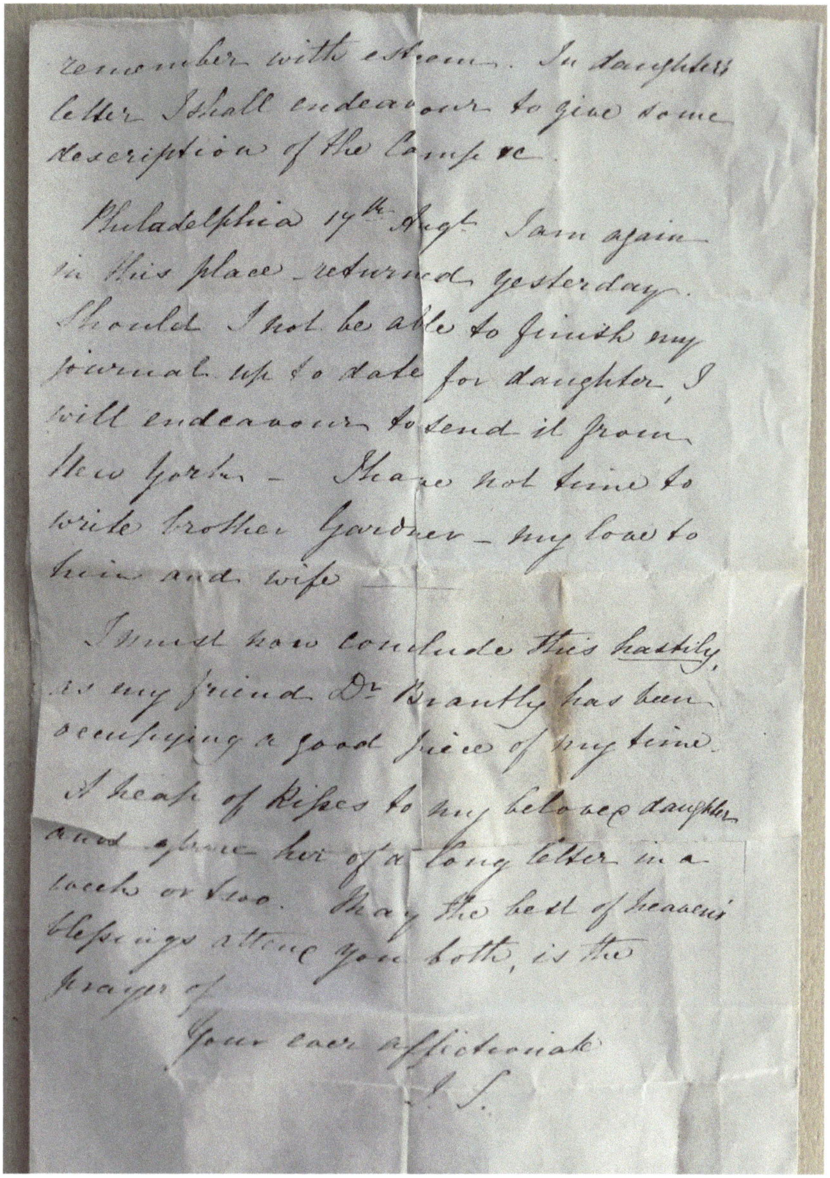

remember with esteem. In daughters letter I shall endeavour to give some description of the camp &c.

Philadelphia 17th Augt. I am again in this place - returned yesterday. Should I not be able to finish my journal up to date for daughter, I will endeavour to send it from New York - I have not time to write brother Gardner - my love to him and wife ———

I must now conclude this hastily, as my friend Dr Brantly has been occupying a good piece of my time.

A heap of kisses to my beloved daughter and assure her of a long letter in a week or two. May the best of heaven's blessings attend you both, is the prayer of

Your ever affectionate

J. S.

Page 4 of letter

Extract from Joshua Tinson letter, with signature

'He will, shall we be able to do this or that. My health is improved,
and I hope improving. I have not been to Boston; am not sure that I
shall be able to go. My love to Mrs Phillippo & family.

Yours affectionately
Joshua Tinson

The handwriting in this letter corresponds with the incomplete section he
wrote in 1838, referencing James Phillippo and signed Joshua Tinson.

Incomplete letter 'of the colonies', referencing the year 1838

'of the colonies (Cape Palmas) just returned from Africa; and I am fully convinced, that whatever incidental, or remote advantages may arise from these societies, they are to say the best of them, as it respects their professed object, adequate to nothing; perfectly useless; and this is as it ought to be. I hope you, Mrs Phillippo & family are all well, and indeed all the mission family. I often think of you, and hope to meet all, at your house in January 1838.

Incomplete letter 'the congregation'

'The congregation in Oliver Street is pretty good, though not so large, I think, as when I was here before, but this is a time when many people leave the city on account of the heat. There is some difference of opinion among the Baptists, respecting the Bible question, of which you have heard. I am told however, that those opposed to the separation form a very small part; a mere fraction of the denomination. Among the number there are some influential men...'

'provoke controversy; but they must understand that I was an abolitionist, and that every particle of me was baptized in hatred to slavery. I told them what had been done, and was still doing in Jamaica, and that the termination of the apprenticeship would be likely to affect their country. Some shook their heads and walked away, others did not like the subject, though they listened; but some would say "come brother Tinson, come tell us all about it; we must think of this matter'

These letters opened a small window into Tinson's life that inspired me to find out more. In the letter he wrote to Eliza, in 1837, he mentioned meeting up with his old friend Colgate, during the period he spent in America.

William Colgate was the founder of the Colgate company. His father, Robert, had been a childhood friend of William Pitt, who was elected Prime Minister of Great Britain in 1783. Pitt warned Robert Colgate that his safety was under threat, as he was an outspoken proponent of the American War of Independence, and advised the family to leave England immediately. The Colgate family emigrated to America and, many years later, William Colgate, became a Christian philanthropist. It was during his time, as a deacon with the Baptist church in New York, that he met Reverend Joshua Tinson.

The fact that William Colgate's father was a friend of William Pitt, and one of my ancestors, George Pretyman Tomline, was also a close friend of Pitt's, leads me to believe the Tinson and Pretyman families may have been known to each other in past generations.

Reverend Tinson died in 1850, and a small section of newspaper, dated March 26 1851, indicates that Eliza and her daughter remained in Jamaica for a few months, before returning to England. They then sailed to Australia in 1855, and settled in Hobart Town.

I recently found records stating that Eliza Tinson and her daughter lived in Patrick Street, Hobart Town. My great great grandparents, Charles and Amy Pretyman, also lived in Patrick Street before moving into Queenborough House in Sandy Bay. This would suggest they were neighbours and could possibly explain the connection between the two families.

My family also inherited a wooden box, from the Tinson family, together with the collection. In 1949, my mum received a letter from her Great Aunt May that refers to the 'workbox' and the collection; 'the thimble case was left to me with workbox by an old lady named Tinson who left your grandfather the cabinet of curios'. My great grandfather was nineteen, when Miss Eliza Tinson died in 1884, at the age of sixty. Auntie May would have been seventeen, in this year which may account for her considering sixty years of age to be 'old'.

Workbox originally belonging to Eliza Tinson

The Thimble is real silver which I bought at
Abbott the Jeweller shop in Murray St
Now pulled down, and gave to my Mother
for a Birthday present & she used it to work
the Pillow shams just a short time before she
died (92 without Spectacles) the Thimble case was
left to me with wardrobe by an old Lady named
Thimble in red case
Finson who left your grandfather the Cabinet of
Curios, she left her money to the Baptist Church,
About £6,000. That is the History of it. Hope you
will keep it in memory of your old Aunt. Also fully yours

Extract from May's letter

Within the workbox containing sewing equipment and documents I found a letter from Auntie May (Amy Mabel Pretyman) relating to this beautiful Victorian Mother-of-pearl and Paua shell calling card case she gave my mother. I have included this image as it relates to the theme of inheriting family heirlooms, my ancestors and the collection of shells.

Mother-of pearl and Paua shell card case with a letter from Auntie May to my Mum

Mum also kept two red, oval leather cases containing miniature portraits, inside this workbox. Both portraits appear to be painted on thin wafers of ivory. Behind the portrait of Eliza is an oval piece of paper with a summary of the Tinson family's story, documented in brown ink. I am amazed that the few words on this small piece of paper provide sufficient detail, including historical dates, to explain the early years of the Tinson family and their relocation, from England to Jamaica, to serve as missionaries.

Their history was also typed onto a separate piece of paper, to accompany the travel cases, containing the miniature portraits. I suspect the additional document was intended to protect Eliza's portrait from excessive handling and to avoid the need to remove the portrait to access the story.

Portraits of Eliza and Joshua Tinson and their story

135

Mrs
Eliza Tinson
born at Shortwood, Gloces-
tershire. the 2nd of November. 1796
Married at Bristol, the 19th February
1822. Her maiden name was Haine.

She sailed with her husband as a
Baptist Missionary to the island of
Jamaica. 24th March - 1822. -
Returned to England on account of ill
health. January the 30th 1829. Left England
again for Jamaica. 29th Oct: in the same year

This miniature was taken in London
just before her departure, and presented as a token of Maternal affection, to
her only surviving child -
Miss Eliza Helah Tinson -

Who was born in Kingston - Jam-
maica, the 9th of December - 1823.

Came to England with her
Mamma, in 1829. and was
left at School with -
Mrs Saffery,
at Salisbury
Wilts

Story behind Eliza Tinson's portrait

The last paragraph on the typed page explains, 'this miniature was given by Miss Eliza Tinson to Miss Augusta Emma Pretyman with other belongings'. Augusta was affectionately known within my family as 'Auntie Gus' and was my great great aunt, and the first daughter born to Charles and Amy Pretyman, in 1857. She was twenty-seven years old when Miss Tinson died, in 1884 aged sixty.

According to these valuable clues, it would appear that the two families had developed a strong bond of friendship, resulting in Miss Tinson's decision to bequeath some of her treasured items to my ancestors.

My mother placed a white sticker with the number 123 on the outside of the red case. This corresponds with the details she recorded in a book, explaining the origins of various family heirlooms. When I looked up the notes in her book, Mum had written, 'pair of miniatures in red cases, beside the number 123. Reverend Tinson and Mrs Tinson, born 1796. Details on the back of each one – believed to be the owners of shell case or their daughter'. I recall asking Mum if the people in these miniature portraits were related to our family, and the only explanation she could offer was the information on the piece of paper, stating that Miss Tinson had given them to Auntie Gus.

Eliza Helah Tinson's parents commissioned these miniature portraits in 1829, but the artist is unknown. There are no visible identifying marks or signatures, apart from the subjects' identification on the back. The portraits were completed and presented to their daughter in England, in 1829, as 'a token of maternal affection'. This endearing gesture must have been comforting for Eliza, during the time she remained in England, completing her schooling. I imagine Eliza spent many hours gazing at the faces of her parents, and kept these portraits close during the long periods they were separated by vast oceans.

Portrait of Reverend Joshua Tinson revealing pencil marks on jacket

Red oval cases with sticker numbered 123, and oval glass that covers portrait

The portraits measure 7 cm x 4 cm and are covered with thick sections of oval glass to provide additional protection within the travel cases, which are covered with red Moroccan leather. The oval cases have different closing mechanisms. Eliza's has two clasps that swing around to hook into the other section, to secure the two parts, while Reverend Tinson's has a single snap closing mechanism. Both cases have a padded cushion, covered in cream silk fabric, within the top section. Beneath Eliza's portrait and the paper with their story, is a layer of deep-blue velvet fabric, plus two pieces of thick card advertising a business. These serve to fill the space, ensuring a snug fit within the case for the portrait and the glass.

I am fascinated by the fine brush strokes and the technique the artist used to provide definition and texture to the surface of these portraits, in a combination of watercolour and gouache. The application and careful placement of additional layers of paint on the portraits adds definition, contour and texture to the surface, creating another dimension.

When I held the portrait of Joshua Tinson up to the light, to examine the surface, I noticed several fine pencil marks on parts of the black jacket he is wearing. These lines are not evident when directly viewing the portrait. The carefully positioned strokes define the creases and folds of the fabric, and the seams where the sleeve attaches to the body of the jacket. The fine broken brush strokes on his hair and mutton-chop sideburns give a fuzzy effect indicating he had thin wiry hair, and bushy eyebrows above his piercing, benevolent brown eyes.

Joshua Tinson portrait painted in 1829

140

The Revd Joshua Tinson, Baptist Missionary to the Island of Jamaica 1826.

Reverse of Joshua Tinson portrait, revealing transparency of ivory wafer

Joshua Tinson portrait revealing paint technique

The portrait of Eliza has carefully positioned brush strokes on her bonnet (mob hat), which defines the layers and gives the effect of fine fabric with a detailed lace edge. I appreciate the technique the artist used in applying layers of paint to define the contours. Thick layers of dark paint were applied to accentuate her raised curls, and a few carefully positioned strokes of white paint, down the centre of the curls, add dimension. Eliza's hairstyle, with its central parting, curls down the side and the mob hat, were the fashion of the day. Eliza's essence, as the wife of a Baptist missionary, is beautifully captured and her demure expression and bright-blue eyes exude a kind and gentle manner.

Portrait of Mrs Eliza Tinson, painted in 1829

Eliza's gold intaglio   *Eliza's intaglio seal in blue glass*

I also found many other keepsakes in the workbox that contained the miniature portraits, including a miniature gold intaglio. On closer inspection, I noticed the letters of Eliza's name were carved into the blue surface that resembles glass. It was designed as a stamp, to be pressed into a wax seal, to secure a letter, but may also have been worn as a pendant.

Mum's workbox and the hidden letters have given me a greater understanding of the people behind my wonderful shell collection. At every turn, this astounding cabinet divulged more of its treasures.

TIME CAPSULE

hidden stories from the past

Mum's collection of heirlooms also contained other interesting pieces that weren't directly about the Tinsons, but which added to my knowledge of the collection and the era. One such item was a small flat box, containing an irregular piece of white stone and four pieces of paper with handwriting on both sides. Another small, separate piece of paper states that the white stone is a "Piece of Lewis Galdy's Tombstone". The handwriting in the story about Lewis Galdy is consistent with the letters written by Joshua Tinson.

Inscription on the Tombstone of Lewis Galdy Esq.
Green Bay — Jamaica

"Dieu sur tout"

Here lies the body of Lewis Galdy Esq.t who departed
this life at Port Royal the 22.d December 1739 —
aged 80 He was born at Montpelier in France,
but left that country for his religion and came
to settle in this island, where he was swallowed
up in the great earthquake in the year 1692 —

and by the providence of God, was by another
shock thrown into the sea, and miraculously
saved by swimming until a boat took him up.
He lived many years after in great reputation,
beloved by all that knew him, and much
lamented at his death —

Piece of Lewis Galdy's Tombstone

When placed in order, the four pieces of paper describe the following story:

Inscription on the Tombstone of Lewis Galdy Esq., Green Bay Jamaica

"'Dieu sur tout"

Here lies the body of Lewis Galdy Esq., who departed this life at Port Royal the 22ⁿᵈ December 1739 – age 80. He was born at Montpeliar (sic) in France but left that country for his religion and came to settle in this island, where he was swallowed up in the great earthquake in the year 1692 and by the providence of God, was by another shock, thrown into the sea and miraculously saved by swimming until a boat took him up. He lived many years after in great reputation, beloved by all that knew him, and much lamented at his death.'

This discovery had me searching for more information, to add another layer to the fascinating stories that were emerging from deep within this little cabinet of curios.

The devastating earthquake that hit Port Royal, Jamaica, in 1692, was followed by a tsunami and a hurricane, which sank many ships and killed thousands. About half the population of Port Royal died and two thirds of the town sank into the ocean, because of a phenomenon called liquefaction. This occurs when loose water fills sandy soil, such as the sand bank on which Port Royal was built, turning it to liquid sludge and resulting in a loss of strength and stability.

In historical records, Lewis Galdy is referred to as 'The Man who was Buried Twice'. First, the sand swallowed him, as the city sank into the ocean, in 1692 and then he died in 1739, in Port Royal, and was laid to rest at Green Bay, across the water from Port Royal. Apparently, Galdy's tombstone was relocated, years later, to the graveyard of St Peter's Anglican Church. Perhaps he should be known as The Man who was Buried Thrice!

Section of the Trelawny newspaper, printed in Falmouth, Jamaica 1851

As I unfolded the hidden sections of newspapers, I also found articles and letters written to The Editor. This printed material provided yet another thread of information about the collection's origins.

The articles and letters to the editor printed in *The Trelawny and Free Press* publications in Falmouth *and The Watchman and Jamaica Free Press* newspapers, reflect the issues and opinions that were current in Jamaica between 1831 and 1851.

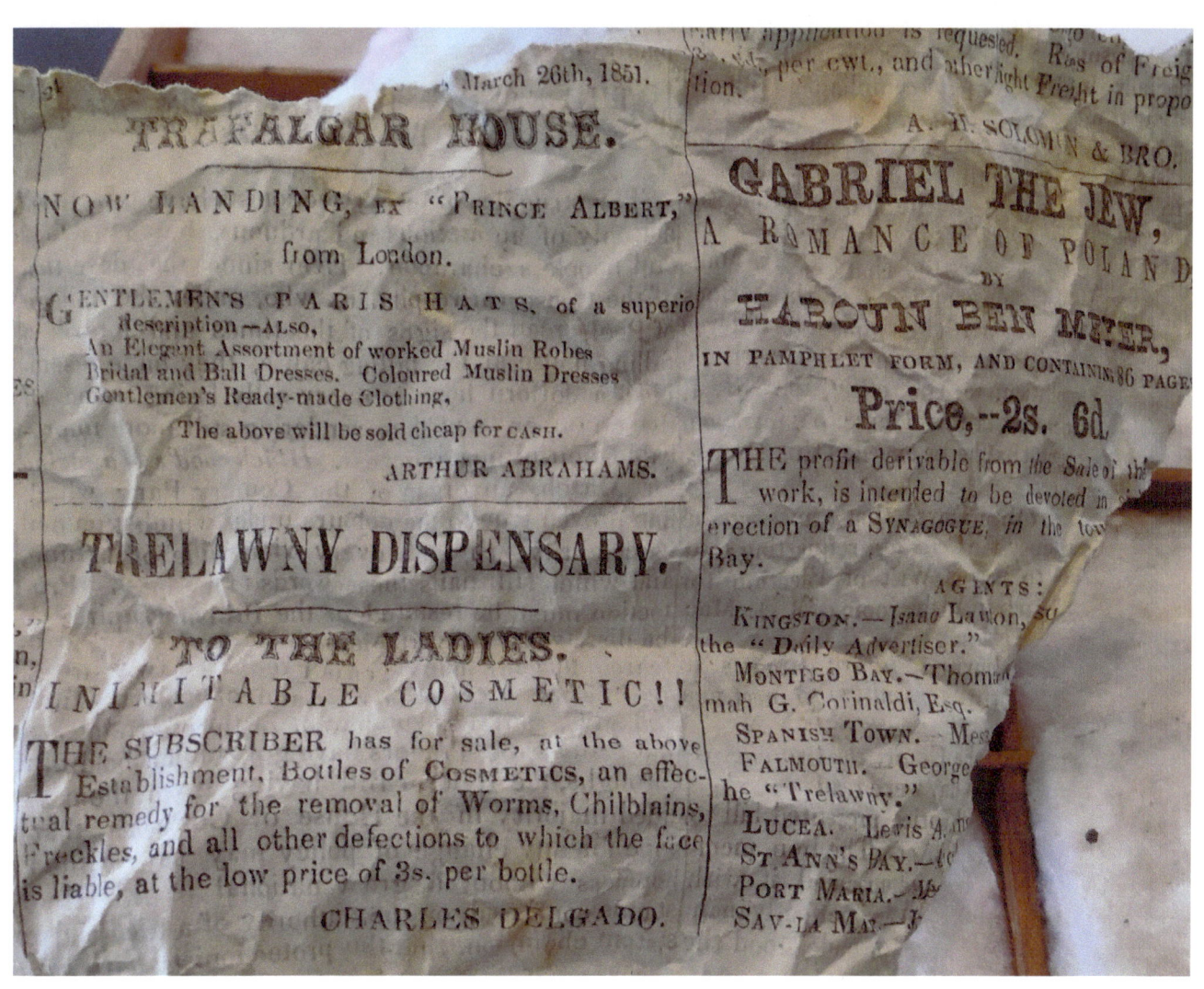

Section of a Trelawny dispensary advertisement, 1851

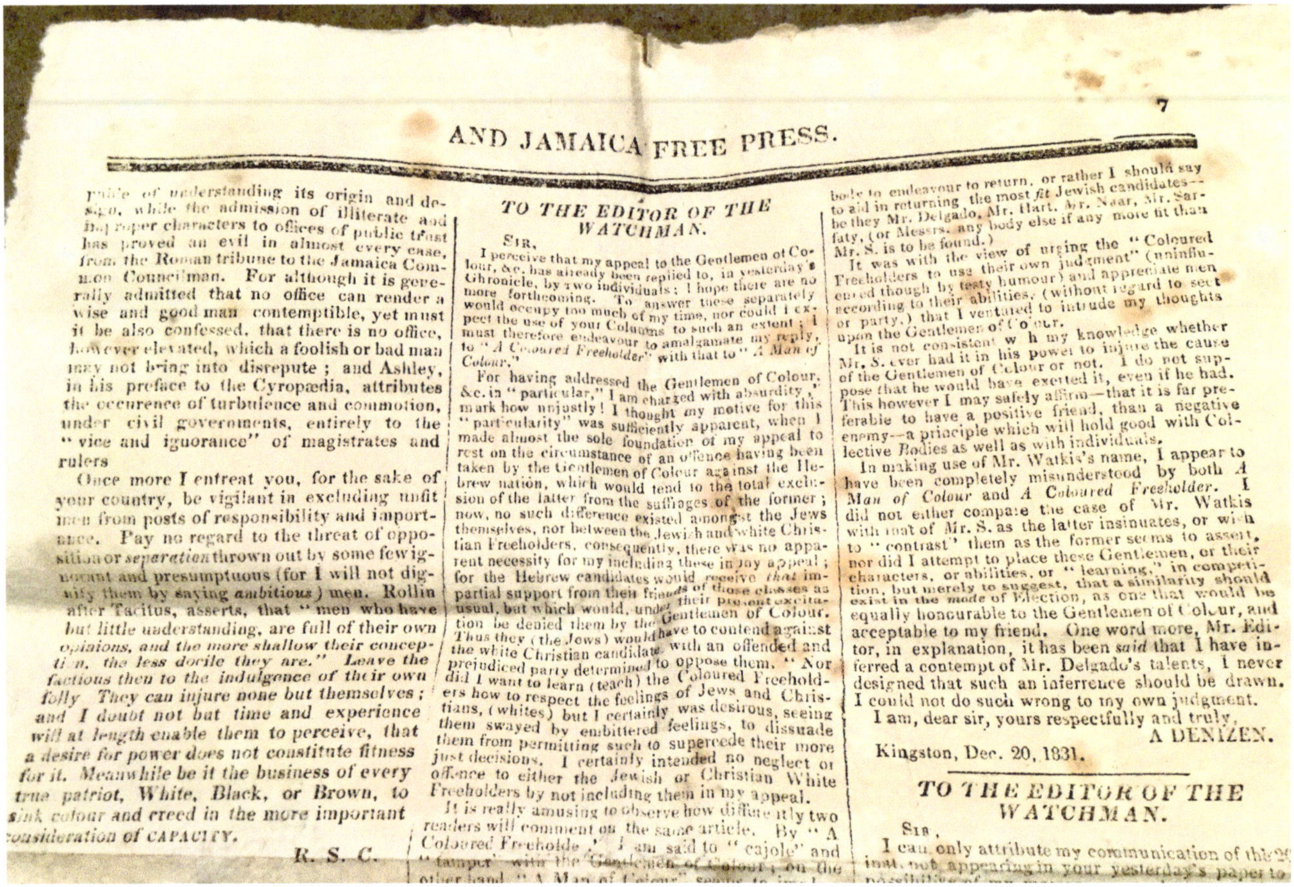

AND JAMAICA FREE PRESS.

7

ratie of understanding its origin and design, while the admission of illiterate and improper characters to offices of public trust has proved an evil in almost every case, from the Roman tribune to the Jamaica Common Councilman. For although it is generally admitted that no office can render a wise and good man contemptible, yet must it be also confessed, that there is no office, however elevated, which a foolish or bad man may not bring into disrepute ; and Ashley, in his preface to the Cyropædia, attributes the occurence of turbulence and commotion, under civil goveroments, entirely to the "vice and iguorance" of magistrates and rulers

Once more I entreat you, for the sake of your country, be vigilant in excluding unfit men from posts of responsibility and importance. Pay no regard to the threat of opposition or *separation* thrown out by some few ignorant and presumptuous (for I will not dignify them by saying *ambitious*) men. Rollin after Tacitus, asserts, that "men who have *but little understanding, are full of their own opinions, and the more shallow their conception, the less docile they are." Leave the factious then to the indulgence of their own folly They can injure none but themselves ; and I doubt not but time and experience will at length enable them to perceive, that a desire for power does not constitute fitness for it. Meanwhile be it the business of every true patriot, White, Black, or Brown, to sink colour and creed in the more important consideration of* CAPACITY.

R. S. C.

TO THE EDITOR OF THE WATCHMAN.

SIR,

I perceive that my appeal to the Gentlemen of Colour, &c. has already been replied to, in yesterday's Chronicle, by two individuals ; I hope there are no more forthcoming. To answer these separately would occupy too much of my time, nor could I expect the use of your Columns to such an extent ; I must therefore endeavour to amalgamate my reply, to "*A Coloured Freeholder*" with that to "*A Man of Colour.*"

For having addressed the Gentlemen of Colour, &c. in "particular," I am charged with absurdity ," mark how unjustly ! I thought my motive for this "particularity" was sufficiently apparent, when I made almost the sole foundation of my appeal to rest on the circumstance of an offence having been taken by the Gentlemen of Colour against the Hebrew nation, which would tend to the total exclusion of the latter from the suffrages of the former ; now, no such difference existed amongst the Jews themselves, nor between the Jewish and white Christian Freeholders, consequently, there was no apparent necessity for my including these in my appeal ; for the Hebrew candidates would receive *that* impartial support from their friends of those classes as usual, but which would, under their present excitation be denied them by the Gentlemen of Colour. Thus they (the Jews) would have to contend against the white Christian candidate with an offended and prejudiced party determined to oppose them. "Nor did I want to learn (teach) the Coloured Freeholders how to respect the feelings of Jews and Christians, (whites) but I certainly was desirous, seeing them swayed by embittered feelings, to dissuade them from permitting such to supercede their more just decisions. I certainly intended no neglect or offence to either the Jewish or Christian White Freeholders by not including them in my appeal.

It is really amusing to observe how differently two readers will comment on the same article. By "A Coloured Freeholder," I am said to "cajole" and "tamper" with the Gentlemen of Colour ; on the other hand "A Man of Colour" seems to ...

bodie to endeavour to return, or rather I should say to aid in returning the most *fit* Jewish candidates—be they Mr. Delgado, Mr. Hart, Mr. Naar, Mr. Sarfaty, (or Messrs. any body else if any more fit than Mr. S. is to be found.)

It was with the view of urging the "Coloured Freeholders to use their own judgment" (uninfluenced though by testy humour) and appreciate men according to their abilities, (without regard to sect or party,) that I ventured to intrude my thoughts upon the Gentlemen of Colour.

It is not consistent with my knowledge whether Mr. S. ever had it in his power to injure the cause of the Gentlemen of Colour or not. I do not suppose that he would have exerted it, even if he had. This however I may safely affirm—that it is far preferable to have a positive friend, than a negative enemy—a principle which will hold good with Collective *Bodies* as well as with individuals.

In making use of Mr. Watkis's name, I appear to have been completely misunderstood by both *A Man of Colour* and *A Coloured Freeholder.* I did not either compare the case of Mr. Watkis with that of Mr. S. as the latter insinuates, or wish to "contrast" them as the former seems to assert, nor did I attempt to place these Gentlemen, or their characters, or abilities, or "learning," in competition, but merely to suggest, that a similarity should exist in the *mode* of Election, as one that would be equally honourable to the Gentlemen of Colour, and acceptable to my friend. One word more, Mr. Editor, in explanation, it has been *said* that I have inferred a contempt of Mr. Delgado's talents, I never designed that such an inferrence should be drawn. I could not do such wrong to my own judgment.

I am, dear sir, yours respectfully and truly,

A DENIZEN.

Kingston, Dec. 20, 1831.

TO THE EDITOR OF THE WATCHMAN.

SIR,

I can only attribute my communication of the 2[illegible] inst. not appearing in your yesterday's paper to ...

The Watchman and Jamaica Free Press newspaper pages, dated 1831

The Watchman and Jamaica Free Press was the first African Jamaican newspaper founded in 1826. It was started by editor, Edward Jordan, in association with Robert Osborn. In 1855, Edward Jordan was the first man of colour to be elected as mayor of his native city, Kingston, and in 1860, he was honoured with a knighthood.

TO THE EDITOR OF THE WATCHMAN.

SIR,

A variety of circumstances occurred to prevent my seeing, before yesterday, your paper of the 26th ult. containing various details of Mr. Maurice Jones, respecting the above road. If his Honour never signed the petition, as he asserted, I give him credit for his honesty, as it affords proof that he did not mean to countenance this humbug with his name. What a pity, that with such delicate feelings, he presented it to the House of Assembly and prayed for the money. I never said that his Honour had left the petition at the *Clerk of the Peace's Office*; therefore there was no necessity for him to deny what he was not accused of. I mentioned "the *Clerk of the Vestry*," who is in many respects under the controul of Mr. Jones. I copy what follows from the Royal Gazette of the 23d October, 1830.

"Portland, October 18, 1830.

"NOTICE IS HEREBY GIVEN.
That the petition, to be presented to the Hon. House of Assembly, praying their aid for the purpose of working the road from Port Antonio to the Portland Gap, is lodged at the Vestry Office for the signatures of the inhabitants.

"By order,
"R. W. Sherwood,
Clerk of the Vestry."

This is not a matter of accommodation between Mr. Sherwood, a resident at Port Antonio, and the framer of the petition. The notice is inserted by Mr. Sherwood, in his quality of Clerk of the Vestry, and *by order?*

The day, 18th October, 1830 was a Vestry day, and his Honour never misses a Vestry. But supposing that he was not present, the *order* came from the Vestry, to whom the jobber presented that petition, artfully concocted as it was, requesting the signature of those who were present. As no body cared about it, many (not all) subscribed their names, and it was moved and agreed to advertise it for signatures; that advertisement was inserted three consecutive weeks in the Royal Gazette. Can Mr. Jones say that he did not see it, that he never inquired about that petition? Can he honestly say that the subject of that road was never mentioned to him, he being intimate with the jobber— *credat judeas!* (1)

not jobbers tendering—a thing they cannot possibly do, without knowing in what condition the road or track is.

Here, probably, Mr. Jones will say "does the supposed favourite jobber know more?"

To this I answer—his Honour, in the very first days of the sitting of the House of Assembly, presented a petition from Mr. Malabre, praying to be remunerated for the loss of a negro *when working on the Portland Gap Road.* Is it not plain by this petition that some work has been done on that road, without *being advertised* for, and that there are some persons initiated into the mystery connected with this road. Is this collusion? Let Mr. Malabre apply to the person or persons who employed him, and not to the country.

I do most solemnly declare, Mr. Editor, that I bear no enmity to Mr. M. Jones, and that he never gave me cause for any. I voted for him at the last election, although most strongly solicited not to do so. I understand that in the *domestic circle* he and his family are most amiable, the present discussion has nothing to do with the private man. In his public character his Honour has behaved with an ill suited vanity, and I might say arrogance; hence the many enemies he has made in a parish, where, 45 years ago, he acted in the mo[s]t menial capacity, (and there are many still living who know it,) thus verifying the axiom, "that where a man, by fortune's frolic, has been raised to a situation to which he had no pretension by birth or education, vanity turns his head and he becomes quarrelsome and overbearing." he becomes quarrelsome and overbearing. Well had it been for Mr. Jones if he had remembered the advice given by Don Quixotte, (who was a good judge of morals,) to his *Squire*, Sancho Panca, when appointed governor of Barataria. (3.)

I am, Mr. Editor, your obedient Servant,
ARGUS.

(1) *I have not said all that I know respecting the jobber and the job, because some communications have been made to me confidentially.*

(2) *See the just objections made by a jobber from St. George's in the Watchman of the 23rd November. The Surveyor, who said that he would not undertake the work, has publicly declared that he job is to be given without any track.*

(3) *In your new, unexpected situation, beware of being proud; recollect that you owe it to chance and not to your merit; and do not forget that in your youth you were a hog-herd; if you do not lose sight of it, nobody will be induced to bring it back to your memory.*

22 Sch. ...

H.M.S. Blanche, Port Royal, Dec. ...

I beg to inform you, for the information of the Merchants of Kingston, that a vessel of war will sail from hence about the 26th or 27th inst. for the purpose of carrying the mail to St. Jago de Cuba.

I have the honour to be, Sir, your humble servant,
A. FARQUHAR, Commodore.

To his Honour the }
Mayor of Kingston. }

** *The sailing of His Majesty's Packet Mutine, is postponed till Saturday the 31st inst.*

Letter Bags at the Commercial Buildings.
Kanhawn, St. Jago de Cuba
Whale, New Orleans
Dash, Halifax
Volador, Havana

PASSENGERS ARRIVED.

In the Lucy Ann (at Port Maria)—Mrs. Sampson and child and Mr. Rogers.

In the Margaret (at ditto)—Mr. Thompson.

In the Lawrence—Charles Nicholas Palmer, Esq. Mr. Forsyth, Mr. Castello, Mr. Rexah, Wm. Banks, Esq and servant.

DIED.

In Montego-Bay, on the 2d inst. Henry, son of the late Henry Fray, Esq. and on Thursday, Mr. ... Simpson, school-master, and Miss Sarah Highat.

At Fontabelle estate, in Trelawny, on the ... inst. aged 4 years, Samuel, son of Mr. William Atterbury.

At Morant Bay, on the 6th inst. at the very advanced age of 107 years, Mrs. Elizabeth Henderson.

On the 16th Duncan M'Kenzie, Esq. late Colonel of the St. Thomas in the East Regiment, much and deservedly regretted. His remains were interred with military honours.

Police Office, Kingston
November 4, 1831.

To Shopkeepers, &c.

NOTICE is hereby given, That under the present Slave Law, Shops of every description must be closed by the hour of ELEVEN in the Forenoon of SUNDAYS, and that only Druggists Shops, Taverns, and Lodging Houses, may be opened, and the sale of Fresh Meat, Fish, or Milk, permitted between the hours of Divine Service.

The several Negro Markets will be closed and every person taken up who may be found vending Goods about the Street after that hour.

ANTHONY GUTZMER,
Police Officer

Section of The Watchman, dated 1831

Police Office, Kingston
November 4, 1831.

To Shopkeepers, &c.

NOTICE is hereby given, That under the present Slave Law, Shops of every description must be closed by the hour of ELEVEN in the Forenoon of SUNDAYS, and that only Druggists Shops, Taverns, and Lodging Houses, may be opened, and the sale of Fresh Meat, Fish, or Milk, permitted between the hours of Divine Service.

The several Negro Markets will be closed and every person taken up who may be found vending Goods about the Street after that hour.

ANTHONY GUTZMER,
Police Officer

The death of Sir George Arthur, 1ˢᵗ Baronet KCH Lieutenant Governor of Van Diemen's Land, from 1823 to 1837, was announced in a newspaper article, and these dates correspond to the period when Reverend Joshua Tinson and his wife resided in Jamaica.

I found newspaper sections, published in England and Tasmania, in the bases of a few of the compartments. These provided a reference, to help me determine the movements of the collection. I believe the natural specimens that Tinson collected in Jamaica may have been wrapped in newspaper and stored in boxes, to protect them during his wife and daughter's return to England after his death, in 1850, and when they moved to Hobart Town, in 1855. The layers of folded newspapers, from Jamaica and England, were placed within the same drawers, alongside pieces from the local newspaper in Hobart Town.

I have concluded that my great-grandfather, Ernest Henry Pretyman, most likely acquired the cabinet to display the specimens he had inherited, and that he was instrumental in modifying the spaces to create the final display. The cabinet may have been designed specifically for collectors to display butterflies, insects or a range of other items, as this was a popular pastime in the colonial era.

gregor.

SIR GEORGE ARTHUR.—We regret to announce the death, on the 19th instant, of Lieutenant-General the Right Hon. Sir George Arthur, Bart., K. C. H. D. C. L., at his residence, in Gloucester-square, Hyde-park, after a long and painful illness. Sir George Arthur entered the army in 1804, served in Sir James Craig's expedition to Italy in 1806; proceeded in the following year to Egypt, and was engaged in the attack on Rosetta, and wounded in the right arm severely. He served in Sicily under Sir James Kempt. In 1809 he was employed in the attack on Flushing, and being then on out post duty, was ordered to check the advance of the French force, which he effected, and was again wounded. He was thanked in general orders, and appointed Deputy-Assistant-Adjutant-General. He subsequently served as Military Secretary to General Sir George Don, when Governor of Jersey. He afterwards joined his regiment in the West Indies, and was selected by the Duke of Manchester, then Governor of Jamaica, as Lieutenant-Governor of Honduras, which government he administered for eight years. Being appointed Lieutenant-Governor of Van Diemen's Land in 1823, he remained in that colony twelve years. On his return to England he was created a Knight Commander of the Royal Hanoverian Guelphic Order, and was selected by Her Majesty's Government in 1837 to proceed to Upper Canada as Lieutenant-Governor, where he remained until the union of the Canadas in 1841. He was created a baronet on his return to England, and was a few months afterwards appointed Governor of the presidency of Bombay. Ill health obliged him to resign the appointment in 1846; but during the time in which he was at Bombay, the Court of Directors appointed, and Her Majesty's Government sanctioned, his being nominated to succeed Lord Hardinge, as Governor-General of India, in the event of that nobleman's death or resignation. His return to England prevented him from deriving any advantage from this high honour. Sir George married Eliza Orde Usher, second daughter of Lieutenant-General Sir Sigismund Smith, Royal Artillery, and is succeeded in his baronetcy by his son, Frederick Leopold.—*Atlas, September 23.*

A TRAVELLER'S IMPRESSIONS OF SEBASTOPOL.— M. Kohl who visited the Crimea about ten years

Announcement of Sir George Arthur's death, in 1854

154

Sir George Arthur - We regret to announce the death, on the 19th instant of Lieutenant-General the Right Hon. Sir George Arthur, Bart., K.C.H.D.C.L., at his residence, in Gloucester-square, Hyde-park, after a long and painful illness. Sir George Arthur entered the army in 1804, served in Sir James Craig's expedition to Italy in 1806; proceeded in the following year to Egypt, and was engaged in the attack on Rosetta, and wounded in the right arm severely. He served in Sicily under Sir James Kempt. In 1809 he was employed in the attack on Flushing, and being then on out post duty, was ordered to check the advance of the French force, which he effected, and was again wounded. He was thanked in general orders, and appointed Deputy-Assistant-Adjutant-General. He subsequently served as Military Secretary to General Sir George Don, when Governor of Jersey. He afterwards joined his regiment in the West Indies, and was selected by the Duke of Manchester, then Governor of Jamaica, as Lieutenant-Governor of Honduras, which government he administered for eight years. Being appointed Lieutenant-Governor of Van Diemen's Land in 1823, he remained in the colony twelve years. On his return to England he was created a Knight Commander of the Royal Hanoverian Guelphic Order, and was selected by Her Majesty's Government in 1837 to proceed to Upper Canada as Lieutenant-Governor, where he remained until the union of the Canadas in 1841. He was created a baronet on his return to England, and was a few months afterwards appointed Governor of the presidency of Bombay. Ill health obliged him to resign the appointment in 1846; but during the time in which he was at Bombay, the Court of Directors appointed, and Her Majesty's Government sanctioned, his being nominated to succeed Lord Hardinge, as Governor-General of India, in the event of that nobleman's death or resignation. His return to England prevented him from deriving any advantage from this high honour. Sir George married Eliza Orde Usher, second daughter of Lieutenant-General Sir Sigmund Smith, Royal Artillery, and is succeeded in his baronetcy by his son, Frederick Leopold-Atlas, September 23.

SHIPPING INTELLIGENCE.

ARRIVED AT PORT-ROYAL.

Dec. 21 Sch. Christian, Hawkins   Honduras, 35 days wood

22 H. M. P. Barque Mutine, Lieut. Pawle   Carthagena

Sch. Seaflower, Dove   Willmington, N.C. 22 days general cargo

23 H.M.S Racehorse, Williams   Chagres, 11 days

Brig Lawrence, ——   New York, 22 days general cargo

Sch. Maria, Catalina   Carthagena, 14 days corn

SAILED FROM PORT-ROYAL.

Dec. 21 Ship Black River Packet, Baker   Black River

Brig Margaret, M'Donald   Honduras
Sch. Sir Lawrence Halsted, Ferres   Choco
—— Nancy, Cray   ditto
Sloop Enterprize, Symmonett   Carthagena
Sch. Polly, Durrant   Rio de la Hache
—— Venzuelo, Arostiqui   Coro
22 Sch. Alpha, Stewart   St. Jago de Cuba

H.M.S. Blanche, Port-Royal, Dec. 21, 1831.

Sir,

I beg to inform you, for the information of the Merchants of Kingston, that a vessel of war will sail from hence about the 26th or 27th inst. for the purpose of carrying the mail to St. Iago de Cuba.

I have the honour to be, Sir, your humble servant.

A FARQUHAR, Commodore.

To his Honour the }
Mayor of Kingston. }

** *The sailing of His Majesty's Packet Mutine, is postponed till Saturday the 31st inst.*

Letter Bags at the Commercial Buildings.

Kanhawn, St. Jago de Cuba
Whale, New Orleans
Dash, Halifax
Volador, Havana

PASSENGERS ARRIVED.

In the Lucy Ann (at Port Maria)—Mrs. Sampson and child and Mr. Rogers.
In the Margaret (at ditto)—Mr. Thompson.
In the Lawrence—Charles Nicholas Palmer. Esq. Mr. Forsyth, Mr. Castello, Mr. Rexah, Wm. Banks, Esq and servant.

156

But now for the incident. This rough and ungainly piece of humanity had, as is often the case, a daughter of surpassing beauty—she had her father's features, but they were softened down to the truly feminine, and, as may be supposed, she had no lack of admirers. But there was one, among them all, who was madly in love with her, not figuratively, but, as the event proved, in reality. Hope of realisation, he could have none; but he 'hoped against hope'—she was his very life, and, waking or sleeping, her presence was ever before him. He knew it was all in vain, for he was a *convict*, and immeasurable indeed was the distance between the daughter of the Governor and a degraded and despised convict. Months had passed; but each glimpse he had of her only served to deepen his infatuation.

And now occurred one of those wondrous that 'truth is stranger than fiction,' and which seemed events, which has so often verified the old saying to Reynolds (for that was the convict's name) the realisation of his heart's desire. The Governor had in his posession, a cabinet of exquisite workmanship, the gift of the Spanish Monarch, as a memorial of his bravery in cutting out a French sloop-of-war, while at anchor in the Port of Barcelona, then held by the enemy. This cabinet the Governor highly prized. It so happened, that either at or on the way back from one of his picnics at Battery Point, the key was lost; search was made for it, but no key could be found. The lock was of peculiar construction, and it appeared impossible to open the cabinet by any other means than by forcing the lock, and thus irretrievably damaging this gift of Royalty. At the last moment, it was reported to the Governor that there was one man in the island who might possibly succeed in picking the lock without in any way disfiguring the cabinet. It was just on his return from brewing and imbibing his favorite beverage when this was told him, and he ordered the man instantly brought into his presence.

'But now for the incident. This rough and ungainly piece of humanity had, as is often the case, a daughter of surpassing beauty – she had her father's features, but they were softened down to the truly feminine, and, as may be supposed, she had no lack of admirers. But there was one, amongst them all, who was madly in love with her, not figuratively, but, as the event proved, in reality. Hope of realisation, he could have none; but he 'hoped against hope' – she was his very life, and, waking or sleeping, her presence was ever before him. He knew it was all in vain, for he was a convict, and immeasurable indeed was the distance between the daughter of the Governor and a degraded and despised convict. Months had passed; but each glimpse he had of her only served to deepen his infatuation.

And now occurred one of those wondrous that "truth is stranger than fiction," and which seemed events, which has so often verified the old saying to Reynolds (for that was the convict's name) the realisation of his heart's desire. The Governor had in his possession, a cabinet of exquisite workmanship, the gift of the Spanish Monarch, as a memorial of his bravery in cutting out a French sloop-of-war, while at anchor in the Port of Barcelona, then held by the enemy. This cabinet the Governor highly prized. It so happened, that either at or on the way back from one of his picnics at Battery Point, the key was lost; search was made for it, but no key was found. The lock was of peculiar construction, and it appeared impossible to open the cabinet by any other means than by forcing the lock, and thus irretrievably damaging this gift of Royalty.

At the last moment, it was reported to the Governor that there was one man in the island who might possibly succeed in picking the lock without in any way disfiguring the cabinet. It was just on his return from brewing and imbibing his favorite beverage when this was told him, and he ordered the man be instantly bought into his presence.'

What a shame this is where this story ends, as I am left wondering what happened, and was the convict, referred to in this article, a man named William Reynolds, who was aged twenty-one years in 1829 and who was convicted of stealing a lamp?

The article in image #167 is from Christmas 1859, and appears to be from the publication, 'Walch's Literary Intelligence, as the name WALCH appears at the top of the section of newspaper. I was able to piece together the details of the story, despite the missing words at the beginning of each line. The story is titled 'Love's Labour Lost: An Incident in Tasmanian History'.

'Love reigns not in a prince's breast alone, but in a prisoner's heart may have her throne. It is now nearly half a century since the incident which I am about to chronicle took place, and I dare say there are but a few in the colony at the present day who can recall associations of so remote a period. Many and varied have been the personages who have figured on the stage of this Island as representatives of Royalty – soldiers, sailors, and civilians, gentlemen and the very opposite, tyrants and protectors – each at different periods have had their day, and have exercised their influence, for good or evil, over the destinies of this land.

Perhaps, of all these, not one has made so strange an appearance, as he, whom I am about to introduce. His manner of entrance into Hobart Town denoted the man. The weather, being warm, when he landed, he carried his coat on his arm, and thus presented himself the 'new Governor.' Once seen, he never could be forgotten. His countenance was strongly marked, and with great delight was, by a peculiar motion of the scalp, throw the forehead into comical contortions, and likewise distort his features, so as to either terrify or'

At this point, the printed information on this torn piece of paper ends, and unfortunately I did not find any other sections of newspaper to continue the story.

LOVE'S LABOUR LOST:
AN INCIDENT IN TASMANIAN HISTORY.

Love reigns not in a prince's breast alone,
But in a prisoner's heart may have her throne.

is now nearly half a century since the incident
hich I am about to chronicle took place, and I dare
y there are but few in the colony at the present day
ho can recall associations of so remote a period.
any and varied have been the personages who have
ured on the stage of this Island as representatives
f Royalty—soldiers, sailors, and civilians, gentlemen
nd the very opposite, tyrants and protectors—each
different periods have had their day, and h ve ex-
cised their influence, for good or evil, over the des-
ies of this land.

Perhaps, of all these, not one has made so strange an
pearance, as he, whom I am about to introduce.
s manner of entrance into Hobart Town denoted the
. The weather, being warm, when he landed, he
ied his coat on his arm, and thus presented himself
e 'new Governor.' Once seen, he never could be
tten. His countenance was strongly marked, and
reat delight was, by a peculiar motion of the scalp,
row the forehead into comical contortions, and
wise distort his features. so as to either terrify or

many
Gove
thoug
father
punis
work
Port
" I
ing
(Rey
locks
sam
the
F
serv
'
an
the
su
ai
b
c
e

#167 *Love's Labour Lost: An Incident in Tasmanian History*

ughed at as a fool. He was asked when and
ot it, and his tale was, that a wild-looking
called himself the son of the Governor—
rmed he had married his daughter—had given
n exchange for ammunition, and that he said
nd it in the bed of a creek, away to the west-
hen the discovery of gold in the neighbouring
as an established fact, the shepherd's gold,
ale he had told about it, was brought to the
n of many, and search was made for him,
dings could be procured. So the matter now

rd in conclusion. There is a party now
rting to the westward, to discover the pre-
l. Let them try to find out the haunt of
han, if he yet be living; and, no doubt, he
them the desired place. He *may* turn out
ng-lost Reynolds—
WHO KNOWS!

Long-lost Reynolds article

Another incomplete snippet from a newspaper refers to Reynolds, a
convict and, sadly, some of the words in the left column are missing.
As these sections of newspaper were only intended to form wads
of packing, to fill the compartments of the shell collection, I can
forgive them for only giving me a hint of these stories.

Another fascinating section of newspaper refers to a story about, Cetshwayo kaMpande, the 'Zulu King' (1873–1879). During his visit to London, he stayed at 18 Melbury Road- This man, who was described as a noble savage, met with Queen Victoria and the Prime Minister. In a photo taken in 1882 Cetshwayo wore his isicoco (a traditional head ring worn by Zulu men) but adopted Western dress. He died in 1884.

when it was ... at last, time, I insisted that he must retire, but as a climax to the day's festivity I made the King a present of a magnum of champagne. His Majesty, it seemed to us, had already a very complete outfit in the shape of liquor, and this magnum was to be reserved till next day. Cetewayo's eyes were fascinated by the magnum. 'Why not drink it now?' he asked through his interpreter. 'You have had enough; we will keep it for you till to-morrow.' 'But if you leave it here they will get up in the night and drink it,' pointing to his attendant chiefs, *one* of whom commanded at Rorke's Drift and the other at Isandula. It was in vain that we protested. We would put it out of their reach. 'Let me take care of it,' said the King. 'But you will drink it,' we said, 'and you have already had enough, and more than enough.' 'No, no,' he persisted. 'I will take good care of it. But I must take it with me to my bedroom; *it* is not safe elsewhere." So at last, after making him promise in the most solemn fashion a Zulu could that he would not draw the cork, we allowed him to carry it off with him to his bedroom. He went out of the room *hugging* the magnum as if it were a precious child. A few minutes afterwards as I went upstairs I saw the *big* bottle standing outside Cetewayo's door drained to the last drop. The temptation had been too much for him. How he found room for the four quarts of champagne after all his libations I cannot imagine. Next day, it is not surprising to learn, His Majesty had a bad cold and could not appear.

"It is some consolation to me to reflect, now that the King's eventful life is over, that probably no period was happier than that ... during which he was under my care at some ... road. The Government was ...

Newspaper article re Cetshwayo the 'Zulu King'

163

'When it was past the King's usual bedtime, I insisted that he must retire, but as a climax to the day's festivity I made the King a present of a magnum of champagne. His Majesty, it seemed to us, had already a complete outfit in the shape of liquor, and this magnum was to be reserved till the next day. Cetewayo's eyes were fascinated by the magnum. 'Why not drink it now? He asked through his interpreter. 'You have had enough; we will keep it for you till to-morrow.' 'But if you leave it here they will get up in the night and drink it,' pointing to his attendant chiefs, one of whom commanded at Rorke's Drift and the other at Isandula.

It was in vain that we protested. We would put it out of their reach. 'Let me take good care of it' said the King. 'But you will drink it we said, and you have already had enough, and more than enough.' 'No, no,' he persisted. 'I will take good care of it. But I must take it with me to my bedroom; it is not safe elsewhere.'

So at last, after making him promise in the most solemn fashion a Zulu could that he would not draw the cork, we allowed him to carry it off with him to his bedroom. He went out of the room hugging the magnum as if it were a precious child. A few minutes afterwards as I went up-stairs I saw the big bottle standing outside Cetewayo's door drained to the last drop. The temptation had been too much for him. How he found room for the four quarts of champagne after all his libations I cannot imagine. Next day, it is not surprising to learn, His Majesty had a bad cold and could not appear. It is some consolation to me to reflect, now that the King's eventual life is over, that probably no period was happier than that during which he was under my care at Melbury Road. The Government was in some doubt as to what to do with its savage guest, when the happy thought struck Lord Kimberley that I, who provide for all men, might provide for Cetewayo.'

Unfortunately, I was unable to complete the story, as the paper was torn, and no other pieces of newspaper were found within the other compartments of this cabinet that continued the tale.

Newspaper sections from The Tasmanian Tribune 1875-76

...nt to the treaty granting to our ...bject ...
right of search of vessels hoisting ...e ...
flag.—Sir T. F. Buxton then moved ...merican
Massie seconded the adoption and pr...g of the
report; after which, the Hon. and Rev. ...Baptist
Noel moved and the Rev. W. Arthur seconded—
"That this meeting deems it of the utmost importance at this crisis to re-affirm the fundamental
principle of the anti-slavery movement, that 'slave-
holding is a sin and a crime before God,' and that
its speedy extinction is devoutly to be desired on
the highest grounds of religion and humanity." Mr.
C. Buxton, M.P., then proposed the following reso-
lution :—"That, in the opinion of this meeting, the
abolition of slavery, decreed to take place from
and after the 1st of July next, in the Dutch West
India colonies, and in 1876 in all the trans-marine
possessions of Portugal; the emancipation of the
serfs in Russia; the total cessation of the African
slave trade to Brazil and from the Portuguese pro-
vinces in West Africa; the new Slave Trade Treaty
with the United States Government, granting a
right of search; the abolition of slavery in the
district of Columbia; its prohibition for ever in the
territories; the recognition of the negro republics
of Hayti and Liberia, and other measures which
the United States Government has initiated, in fur-
therance of emancipation, claim signal and grateful recognition from the friends of human freedom
in all lands, and are acts calculated to encourage
them to unabated and united efforts to obtain
total and speedy extinction of the slave trade and
of slavery wherever they exist."—Mr. P. Sinclair
seconded the motion, which was unanimously
agreed to, and the meeting separated.

C. Buxton M.P. article re abolition of slavery

Mercury

TUESDAY MORNING, SEPTEMBER 25, 1883.

Drapery Clothing, Etc

ROBERT HEMPSEED,
FAMILY DRAPER,
42, ELIZABETH-STREET,

HAS OPENED HIS FIRST SPRING
SHIPMENT,
TWENTY CASES OF NEW DRAPERY.

3 Cases Dress Goods—Beige Dress Materials, 8d. to 1s.; New Check Beiges, 1s. and 1s. 3d.; Nuns' Veilings, 1s. 3d. and 1s. 6d.; Soft Jumbo Twills, 1s.; Coloured Lustres, 8d. to 1s.

1 Case Black Cashmeres, 1s. 6d. to 4s. 6d.

1 Case Black Alpacas, 9d. to 2s. 6d.

3 Cases New Prints, 6d. to 10d.

1 Case Plain and Figured Sateens, 9d. and 10½d.

3 Cases Women's and Children's Hosiery

2 Cases Lawn Handkerchiefs, Fancy Metal Buttons, Black and Coloured Taffeta Gloves, Bibs, Laces, Little Folks, and Middy Collars

ase Black and Coloured Velveteens, to 5s.

Medical

A. P. MILLER,
PHARMACEUTICAL CHEMIST,
Murray-street,

Begs to intimate the receipt, ex "Mylomine," *via* Melbourne, of 21 cases of
DRUGS AND CHEMICALS,
Comprising Howard's Soda, Borax, Sulphate of Quinine, Iodide of Potassium, Bromide of Sodium, Turkey Gum, Myrrh, Bichromate of Potash, Calvert's Carbolic Acid, Gum Camphor, Cyanide of Potassium, Pyrogallic Acid, Hotchkiss' Oil of Peppermint, etc., etc., etc.

For the convenience of medical men and those having the care of Invalids a registry of Nurses and Male Attendants is kept, free of charge.

Nurses are requested to furnish information of change of address, and to report themselves once a month. Those desirous of re-engagement are requested to apply from time to time.

Hobart, September 20, 1883.

The Mercury September 25, 1883, article re Family Draper clothing descriptions and Miller Pharmaceutical Chemist Drugs and Chemicals

he same evening.

By the schooner Nautilus, which arrived in Fremantle a few days ago, we have advices from the North-West Coast settlements to the 14th January. Pearling operations had gone on satisfactorily; but although all concerned have done well, the take of shells will be considerably less than it was last season; exhibiting a decrease of probably as much as 100 tons. About 1200 divers were at work, of whom upwards of 800 were Malays. The aboriginal natives and the islanders agree remarkably well; in fact, sociability between the two races appears to improve, as at each sucessive season they met to recommence operations. Observations made during the present season confirm the supposition that not only does the oyster possess no appreciable power of migration, but that the force of currents has little or no effect on the movements of the mollusc. Banks which were cleared last season were found this year to be so covered with shells that as many as 500 to 600 pairs per day were fished up, while as the bottom became disturbed, more particularly after boisterous weather, others appeared. Embedded in the muddy, gravelly bottom, from time to time, layers of the bivalve became exposed by disturbances in the water caused by ..., and no doubt in some measure ... tion caused by the tides.

Schooner Nautilus article

merce, and in order to swell the profits so considered of our employers, our time is to be abstracted, our faculties deadened, and our nature enervated by an incessant application to business. "Dulce est desipere in loco" is a maxim of wide world application, still our employers cannot or will not, now, see its general adaptability to our case. Business is the cry, and no matter who suffers; let business be advanced! It appears that a certain firm has determined to keep open until eight o'clock for the ensuing summer, and that, seduced by this peccant example, the other firms have resolved to do the same. Thus it follows that as one scabby sheep will infect a whole flock, so one insatiable draper will inoculate all the others with avarice. Now, if it could be clearly shown that this lengthening of shop hours really tended to the financial interests of the employers there might be some excuse for demanding increased labour from assistants. I do not, however, mean by this to acknowledge that employers can morally require those under them to injure themselves either bodily or mentally in their service—there is a certain length beyond which

'Dulce est desipere in loco' article re shop hours

'Found, a Kangaroo Dog, skin dark brown. The owner can have the same by paying all expenses, and applying to F. Holmes, Butcher.

(The kangaroo dog was the first dog breed in Australia, and also known as the Staghound, a hybrid of the Scottish deerhound, and Greyhound, bred as hunting dogs to assist early settlers with supplies of fresh meat, and they also protected livestock).

British and Foreign Items – There are 382,000 domestic servants in London

The last execution of Quakers in Boston took place in 1861

The New York City Government employs 1,000 snow shovelers'

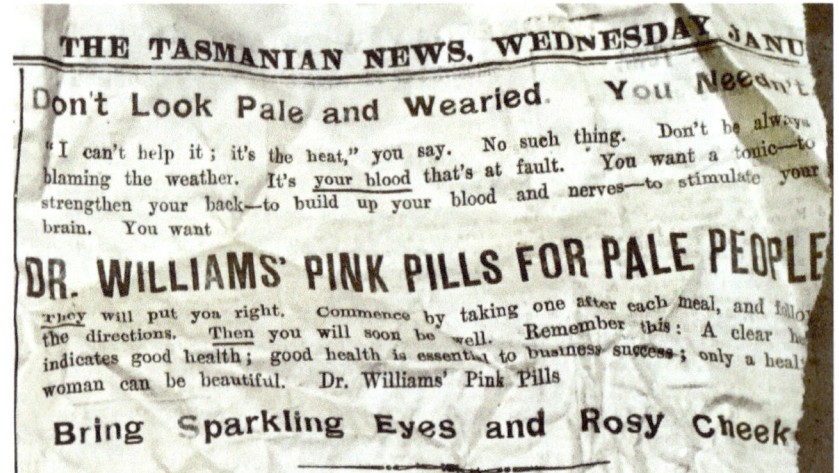

Interesting articles

Pale Girls Made Pretty.

Upon parents rests a great responsibility at the time their daughters are budding into womanhood If your daughter is pale, complains of weakness, is 'tired out' upon the slightest exertion; if she is troubled with headache or backache, pain in the side, if her temper is fitful and her appetite poor, she is in a condition of extreme peril, a fit subject for the most dreaded of all diseases—Consumption. If you notice any of the above symptoms lose no time in procuring Dr Williams' Pink Pills. They will assist the patient to develop properly and regularly; they will enrich the *blood* and restore health's roses to the cheeks; bright eyes and lightness of step will surely follow their use, and all danger of consumption and premature death will be averted.

THE TASMANIAN NEWS.

Publicum bonum privato est præferendum.

WEDNESDAY, JANUARY 11, 1899.

THE ANNUAL CARNIVAL.

A FORTNIGHT hence and Tasmania will, in company with the other colonies, hold high holiday in celebration of the foundation of Australasia. Hobart should on that day be *en fête*, for is it not the national holiday for the Capital, the occasion which has been kept sacred to the devotion of Neptune for more than sixty years? Regatta day in Hobart is what New Year's Day is to the Scotch and Christmas Day to the English; it is the one occasion during the twelve months when friends from all parts of the Island foregather on the slopes of the Domain renewing old acquaintances, or parents and children uniting as in times before the youthful members left the parental home for their own. In days which are past there was some attention given to aquatic events, and interested and excited partisans of the crews followed closely the movements of their favorites. Every ounce put into the ash was rewarded with encouraging cheers, and even when it was palpable to the most prejudiced that no earthly effort could secure a victory, still the unsuccessful ones were urged on to do their utmost. And nobly did they respond to the call made upon them; there was no relaxing of effort until the judge's boat was passed, there was no giving up; no, it was a struggle, desperate in its nature, until the end. But a change has come over the whole. Now-a-days the majority of the thousands who assemble on the Domain do so because it is the fashion and it is a convenient and pleasant picnicking ground. So far as many of them are concerned, the excellent programme annually prepared by the Regatta Association is of not the slightest consequence; they are not concerned whether there are any competitors or not, or whether there is any *vim* among those taking part; they have come out for a pleasant day's amusement and th invariably get it. But thi

The Annual Carnival – Regatta Day in Hobart Wednesday January 11, 1899 article in The Tasmanian News

Wednesday, January 11, 1899

THE ANNUAL CARNIVAL

A fortnight hence and Tasmania will, in company with the other colonies, hold high holiday in celebration of the foundation of Australasia. Hobart should on that day be en fete, for it is not the national holiday for the Capital, the occasion which has been kept sacred to the devotion of Neptune for more than sixty years? Regatta day in Hobart is what New Year's Day is to the Scotch and Christmas Day to the English; it is the one occasion during the twelve months when friends from all parts of the Island foregather on the slopes of the Domain renewing old acquaintances, or parents and children uniting as in times before the youthful members left the parental home for their own. In days which are past there was some attention given to aquatic events, and interested and excited partisans of the crews followed closely the movements of their favourites. Every ounce put into the ash was rewarded with encouraging cheers, and even when it was palpable to the most prejudiced that no earthly effort could secure a victory, still the unsuccessful ones were urged on to do their utmost. And nobly did they respond to the call made upon them; there was no relaxing of effort until the judge's boat was passed, there was no giving up; no, it was a struggle, desperate in its nature, until the end. But a change has come over the whole. Now-a-days the majority of the thousands who assemble on the Domain do so because it is the fashion and it is a convenient and pleasant picknicking ground. So far as many of them are concerned, the excellent programme annually prepared by the Regatta Association is of not the slightest consequence; they are not concerned whether there are competitors or not, or whether there is any vim among those taking part; they have come out for a pleasant day's amusement and they invariably get it.

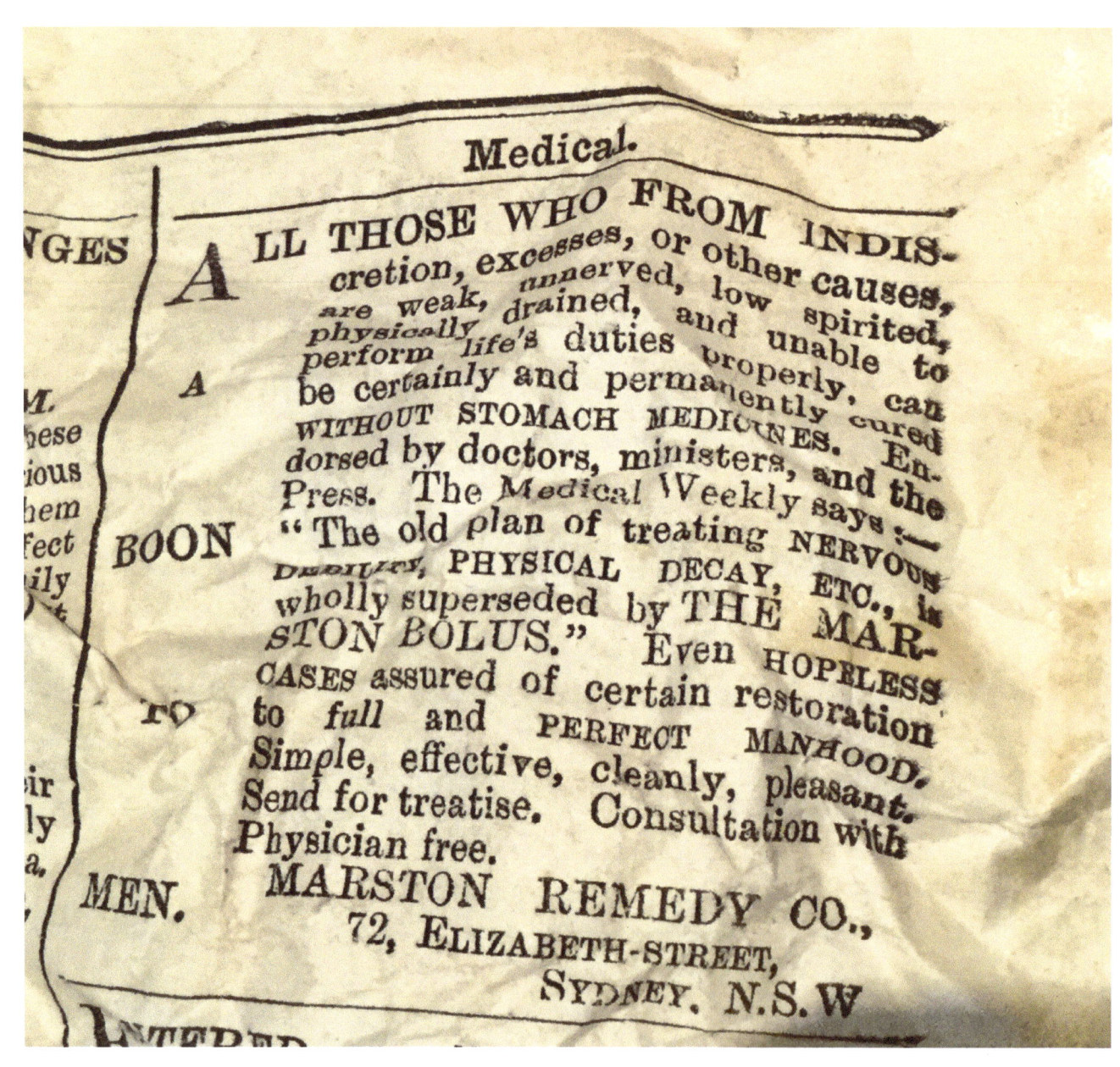

Medical Marston Remedy Co. Sydney advertisement

HORTON COLLEGE near Ross; Rev. F. Neale, President; Mr. W. W. Fox, B.A., Head-master. School duties will be Resumed on THURSDAY, July 24. Vacancies for a few additional Boarders. g472

TASMANIAN ACADEMY, Arthur-street. — Work of the School was RESUMED on 14th July. T. H. BROMFIELD, Principal. g547

MONSIEUR AUJARD Is prepared to give LESSONS In Conversational and Grammatical French.
Address care of the French Consul, 1 Lord's-place, Elizabeth-street, Hobart. g60

School ads: Horton College, Tasmanian Academy and Monsieur Aujard

Excursion to the beautiful Huon River

EXCURSION TO THE BEAUTI-FUL HUON RIVER. Hartz Mountains, Geeveston, Franklin, Shipwrights' Point, Castle Forbes Bay, Long Bay, Peppermint Bay, Oyster Cove, and Channel Ports, by the only

HUON. Specially Built for the Trade. This Favorite and Palatial Passenger and Excursion Steamer makes special Visitors' Trip THURSDAY, 8.30 a.m., returning Friday. Tourists for Geeveston, Mountains, and Lakes carried free from Shipwrights' Point. "Huon's" Trips pronounced the very best in Southern Tasmania. Promenade deck, fine saloon, ladies' cabin, every comfort. Fitzpatrick and Presse. Head office, Brooke street. Tel. 138. 123

BUSH HOTEL, NEW NORFOLK.

The above favourite and well-known Hotel is beautifully situated on the banks of the River Derwent, overlooking some of the grandest views in the Island.

Hot and Cold Baths, Billiards, etc., and all the comforts usually found in first-class houses; also a large garden, beautifully laid out with choice fruit and flowers.

Boats and Fishing Tackle kept for the use of Visitors.

Carriages wait the arrival of the steamer, and convey visitors to the Hotel free of charge.

O. BLOCKEY.

Bush Hotel, New Norfolk

Amusements Soirees, Lectures. Etc.

EXHIBITION BUILDING.

YE OLDE ENGLYSHE FAYRE.

In aide of
YE CRICKET ASSOCIATION'S DEBT,
Under ye patronage of ye Queen's Loyal
Representative
SIR GEO. C. STRAHAN, K.C.M.G.,
C.B., ETC.
THIS AFTERNOON !
THIS AFTERNOON !
GRAND PERFORMANCE FOR
CHILDREN.
SPECIAL PROGRAMME.
Opening 2.30. Commencing 3.
TO-NIGHT ! TO-NIGHT !
Commencing 8. Doors open 7·30.
ADMISSION—ONE SHILLING.
Hon. Sec., J. G. DAVIES.

NEW AND EXTRAORDINARY
NOVELTIES.

1. Ye Olde Maypole Dances.
2. The Dancing Giraffes.
3. The Shadow Pantomime.

First Appearance in Tasmania of
SIGNOR CANNA
Who will perform one of the most
MARVELLOUS AND INDESCRIBA-
BLE PERFORMANCE ON
25 DRUMS.
THE BATTLE OF TEL-EL-KEBIR.
Daylight — Drums

Exhibition Building. Ye Olde Englyshe Fayre

Interesting facts

A. Butterfield's advertisement 1899

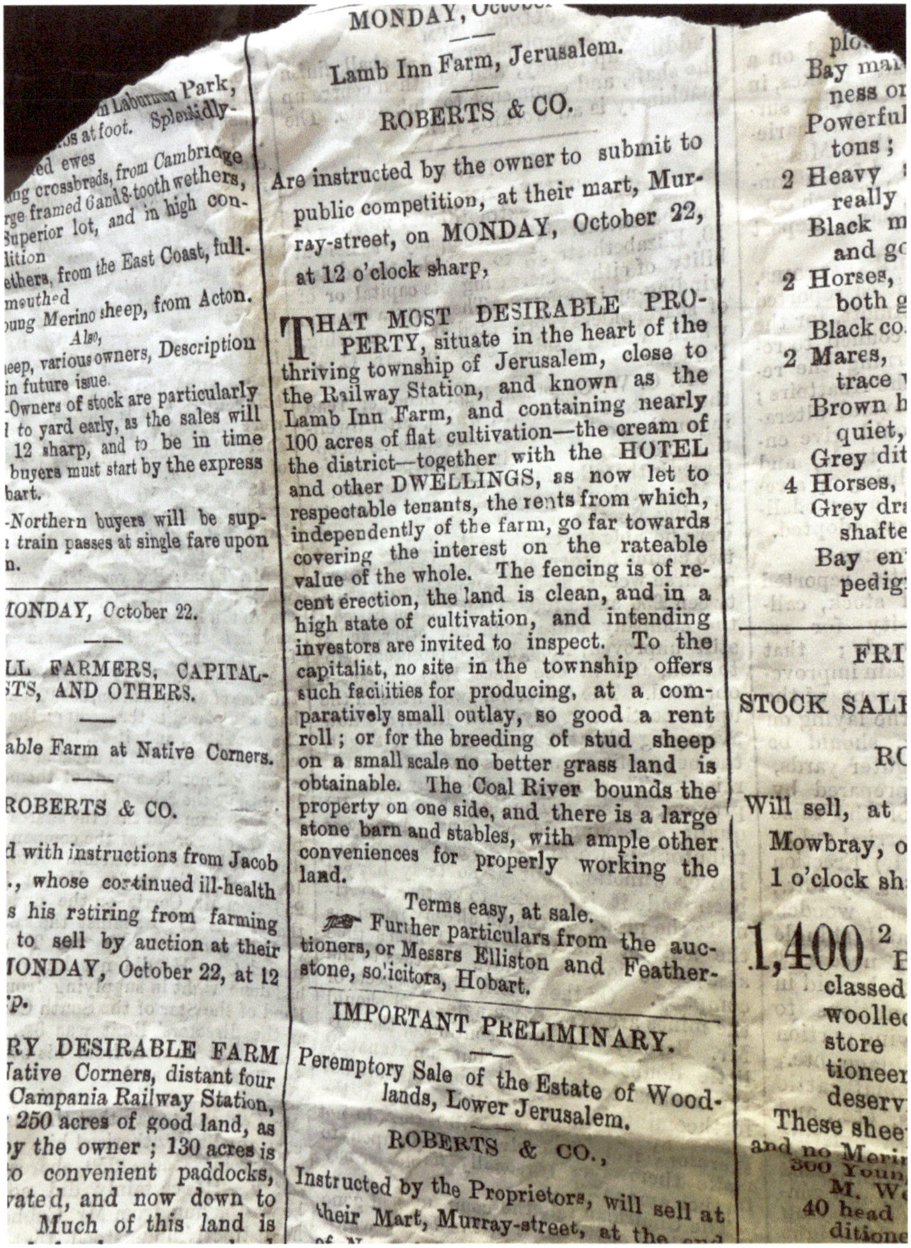

MONDAY, October

Lamb Inn Farm, Jerusalem.

ROBERTS & CO.

Are instructed by the owner to submit to public competition, at their mart, Murray-street, on MONDAY, October 22, at 12 o'clock sharp,

THAT MOST DESIRABLE PROPERTY, situate in the heart of the thriving township of Jerusalem, close to the Railway Station, and known as the Lamb Inn Farm, and containing nearly 100 acres of flat cultivation—the cream of the district—together with the HOTEL and other DWELLINGS, as now let to respectable tenants, the rents from which, independently of the farm, go far towards covering the interest on the rateable value of the whole. The fencing is of recent erection, the land is clean, and in a high state of cultivation, and intending investors are invited to inspect. To the capitalist, no site in the township offers such facilities for producing, at a comparatively small outlay, so good a rent roll; or for the breeding of stud sheep on a small scale no better grass land is obtainable. The Coal River bounds the property on one side, and there is a large stone barn and stables, with ample other conveniences for properly working the land.

Terms easy, at sale.
Further particulars from the auctioneers, or Messrs Elliston and Featherstone, solicitors, Hobart.

IMPORTANT PRELIMINARY.

Peremptory Sale of the Estate of Woodlands, Lower Jerusalem.

ROBERTS & CO.,

Instructed by the Proprietors, will sell at their Mart, Murray-street, at the end

---

(left column fragments)

... n Laburnum Park,
...s at foot. Splendidly-
...d ewes
...ng crossbreds, from Cambridge
...rge framed 6 and 8-tooth wethers,
Superior lot, and in high con-
...lition
...ethers, from the East Coast, full-
...mouthed
...oung Merino sheep, from Acton.
Also,
...eep, various owners, Description
in future issue.
—Owners of stock are particularly
...l to yard early, as the sales will
... 12 sharp, and to be in time
... buyers must start by the express
...bart.
—Northern buyers will be sup-
... train passes at single fare upon
...n.

...ONDAY, October 22.

...LL FARMERS, CAPITAL-
...STS, AND OTHERS.

...able Farm at Native Corners.

...ROBERTS & CO.

...d with instructions from Jacob
..., whose continued ill-health
...s his retiring from farming
... to sell by auction at their
...ONDAY, October 22, at 12
...p.

...RY DESIRABLE FARM
...ative Corners, distant four
...Campania Railway Station,
...250 acres of good land, as
...y the owner; 130 acres is
...o convenient paddocks,
...vated, and now down to
...Much of this land is

(right column fragments)

...plo
Bay mar...
ness or...
Powerful...
tons;
2 Heavy
really
Black m...
and go...
2 Horses,
both g...
Black co...
2 Mares,
trace...
Brown h...
quiet,
Grey dit...
4 Horses,
Grey dr...
shafte...
Bay en...
pedig...

FRI...
STOCK SAL...

RC...

Will sell, at...
Mowbray, o...
1 o'clock sh...

1,400 ...
classed...
woolle...
store...
tioneer...
deserv...
These shee...
and no Meri...
300 Youn...
M. W...
40 head...
ditione...

Lamb Inn Farm, Jerusalem Roberts & Co.

THE
Hobart Town Gazette

PUBLISHED BY AUTHORITY.

HIS Excellency The LIEUTENANT GOVERNOR directs, that all Public Notifications which may appear in this Paper with any Official Signature thereunto affixed, shall be considered as Official Communications made to those Persons to whom they may relate.

BY *Command of His Excellency,*

JOHN BURNETT, *Colonial Secretary*

VOLUME XIII)   SATURDAY, APRIL 26, 1828.   (NUMBER 624

BY His Excellency Colonel GEORGE ARTHUR, Lieutenant Governor of the Island of Van Diemen's Land and its Dependencies.

PROCLAMATION.

WHEREAS, at, and since the primary Settlement of this Colony, various acts of aggression, violence, and cruelty have been, from different causes, committed on the Aboriginal Inhabitants of the Island, by subjects of His Majesty.

AND WHEREAS, for the preventing and punishing such sanguinary, and wicked practices, it was by a certain General Order made by Colonel DAVID COLLINS, (then) Lieutenant Governor of this Island and its Dependencies, at Government-House, Hobart Town, on the 29th day of January, 1810, declared, "that any "Person whosoever, who should offer "violence to a Native, or should, in "cool blood, murder, or cause any of "them to be murdered, should, on "proof being made of the same, be "dealt with, and proceeded against, as "if such violence had been offered or "Murder committed on a civilized "Person:"—AND, it was also, by a certain Proclamation, made and issued by me, as such LIEUTENANT GOVERNOR as aforesaid, at Government House, Hobart Town, on the 29th day of June, 1824, after reciting the command of His Majesty's Government and the injunction of His Excellency The Governor in Chief, that the Natives of this Colony and its Dependencies, should be considered as under British Government Protection, declared, that every violation of the laws, in the Persons, or property of the Natives should be visited with the same punishment, as if committed on the Persons or property of any Settler; and all Magistrates and Peace Officers, and others His Majesty's subjects in this Colony, were thereby strictly required to observe and enforce the provisions of that Proclamation:—AND WHEREAS, the Aborigines did not only defend themselves, and retaliate on the offenders; but did also, subsequently to the Order, and Proclamation aforesaid, and notwithstanding the recital, declarations and requisition mentioned, perpetrate frequent unprovoked outrages on the Persons and property of the Settlers in this Island, and their Servants, being British subjects; and did indulge in the repeated commission of wanton, and barbarous Murders, and other Crimes;—for the repression of which, as also for the prevention of farther offences by either of the said parties, instructions, directions, and injunctions were promulgated for general information, and for the especial guidance of the Civil Authorities, and the Military Forces, by the Government Notices of the 29th November, 1826, and the 29th November, 1827, respectively.

AND WHEREAS, those several measures have proved ineffectual to their objects; and the Persons employed in the Interior of this Island, as Shepherds and Stockkeepers, or on the Coast as Sealers, do still, as is represented, occasionally attack and injure the Aboriginal Natives without any Authority;—and the Aborigines have, during a considerable period of time, evinced, and are daily evincing, a growing spirit of hatred, outrage, and enmity against the subjects of His Majesty, resident in this Colony, and are putting in practice modes of hostility, indicating gradual, though slow advances in art, system, and method, and utterly inconsistent with the peaceable pursuits of Civilized Society, the most necessary arts of human subsistence, or the secure enjoyment of human life.

AND WHEREAS, on the one hand, the security and safety of all who have intrusted themselves to this Country on the faith of British protection, are imperatively required by the plainest principles of justice:—And, on the other hand, humanity and natural equity, equally enforce the duty of protecting and civilizing the Aboriginal Inhabitants.

AND WHEREAS, the Aborigines wander over extensive tracts of this Country, without cultivating, or permanently occupying any portion of it, making continual predatory incursions on its settled Districts, a state of living alike hostile to the safety of the Settlers, and to the amelioration of their own habits, character and condition.

The Hobart Town Gazette 1828

181

My dear mum would be astounded by the history I discovered within her treasure chest, and I am sure she would be thrilled with the images that showcase the essence of nature's beauty. It is unlikely that Joshua or Ernest ever thought that their simple act of using pieces of paper as a foundation, to support their collection, would one day result in the revelations discovered in this time capsule of history.

The gathering of these specimens, no doubt, rewarded Joshua Tinson and my great grandfather with great pleasure and immense satisfaction and I can only imagine their delight each time they found a new seashell to add to the collection. This exquisite display required many years of care, dedication and commitment. I thank Joshua and Ernest, for preserving and protecting these specimens within the darkness of this little chest of drawers, as it ensured that their vibrancy and integrity had not been compromised with the passage of time.

I will be forever indebted to Miss Eliza Tinson, for her decision to bequeath her father's collection to Ernest, who shared their love and appreciation of natural specimens. Ernest Henry Pretyman's contribution to the collection, prior to his death in 1941, is the *pièce de résistance*.

So, in the end, the strangers, who stared back at me from the miniature portraits in their red leather cases, found their way into my heart, and the Tinson family and my great grandfather have earned my deep respect and gratitude for this magnificent collection. It has been a privilege to add my personal touch to the collection. I hope my contribution complements the original display and that Joshua, Ernest and Mum would be pleased with the result. The restoration of this collection has been a labour of love and I am thankful to be the custodian of this remarkable antique heirloom, as it has given me years of ineffable pleasure and immense joy.

BIBLIOGRAPHY

Downing, B. & Mansfield, J. (1960). Tinka and His Friends. (1st ed.), Thomas Nelson, Melbourne.

Dendy, W., Clark, J. & Phillippo, J.M. (1865). The Voice of Jubilee: A Narrative of the Baptist Mission, Jamaica, From Its Commencement, John Snow, London.

Tasmanian Archives: Pretyman Family (NG1012) Series: Photographs and Glass Plate Negatives collected by E.R Pretyman: Image:NS103/1/871

BIOGRAPHY

Christine Robinson was born in Hobart, Tasmania.

After a rewarding four decades of nursing specialising in Neurosurgery, Christine retired to devote her time to research her family's history and write stories about her wonderful travel experiences.

From following the Hippie Trail overland from Kathmandu to London via the Khyber Pass, to living on a Kibbutz in Israel, Christine's life has been a wonderful adventure.

Now living in the idyllic beachside town of Noosa Heads, Christine resides with her adorable companion, Indie, the Westie.

Christine Joy Robinson
(Photo credit: Katja Anton)

'Here is your country. Cherish these natural wonders, cherish the natural resources, cherish the history and romance as a sacred heritage, for your children's children. Do not let selfish men or greedy interests skin your country of it's beauty, it's riches or it's romance'.
Theodore Roosevelt